D1325371

You're planning to turn your lawn over to leeks, grow beans in your borders and sow radishes among your roses — but you're not sure how to go about it. This straightforward, sensible guide will encourage you to go ahead and ensure you make a success of it, whether you're changing over or starting from scratch. The clear, step-by-step pictures accompany a text which is packed with all the practical expertise of a well-known gardening expert. There is no gardening author better qualified to write on this subject than Sheila Howarth, whose first love is the vegetable garden. She shows you how to grow common, everyday vegetables with a most uncommon flavour, and introduces you to less familiar ones that are scarce and expensive to buy or even unobtainable commercially. She guides you towards those vegetables which are most worth growing, tells you exactly how to handle each one and explains ways of storing the surplus. And she gives tips on preparing and cooking some of the lesser known crops so that they reach your table at the peak of perfection.

ISBN 0 85223 074 5

£2.50
NET

Contents

Why and What to Grow

Growing one's own vegetables has three outstanding advantages:

1 Economy The consumer spends less on petrol and does not have to bear the cost of the transport of commercial crops from grower to shop. As against the time spent on cultivation, the consumer's shopping time is saved. Vegetables you buy in shops or from stalls must be sold at a profit, so that both grower and shopkeeper can make a living; the home gardener can produce his vegetables at cost price and in tip-top condition.

2 Convenience The owner of a well-planned vegetable garden has a greengrocer's shop on the spot. No need to think and plan meals ahead; you take your fresh or stored vegetables as and when you need them. No using up that old, tired cauliflower, bought for the weekend for a dish that never got made. Catering for unexpected guests, even on Sunday, is no longer an anguish. Gluts can be dealt with by freezing, bottling, pickling, or used to make chutneys and preserves.

3 Flavour You can choose varieties for their flavour alone, without having to produce those with the biggest crop, as commercial growers do. Shop-bought varieties are rarely for the discriminating palate since they have to put up with the rough and tumble of being picked, sorted, weighed, packed, transported and weighed again before going into your shopping basket. This requires tough skins and constitutions, combined with non-perishable qualities which seldom go hand in hand with flavour and freshness. With the exception of carefully stored root vegetables, freshness is an integral ingredient of flavour.

Selective Planning

Unless you are lucky enough to have plenty of space it is clearly best to concentrate on growing vegetables that your family likes best and those that are expensive or not readily available in shops. Crops which reach the retailer when they are too large and old, such as broad beans, runner beans and peas, and crops which must be cooked as soon as harvested, such as asparagus and sweetcorn, are particularly good value.

HOW MUCH SPACE?

To give some guidance on size, the standard allotment in Britain, 27 m x 9 m (90 ft x 30 ft), can provide enough vegetables, with the exception of main crop potatoes, to keep a family of four supplied throughout the year. A few rows of early potatoes are worthwhile, but main crop ones are heavy on space and liable to a good many diseases.

A smaller plot, 9 m x 3 m (30 ft x 10 ft) would be large enough to grow salads, peas, runner beans, carrots and beetroot for the summer, and for the winter, cabbage, brussels sprouts, sprouting broccoli, leeks and celery.

Another estimate gives 500 m² (600 sq yd) of ground as necessary for *all* the vegetables and salads for a family of four for a whole year. This will take about 230 hours a year to sow, cultivate and harvest properly... depending on your agility, skill and interpretation of 'properly'. If you leave out main crop potatoes, then only 376 m² (450 sq yd) and 210 hours a year will see you through.

Where, How and When to Grow

Vegetables need a *sunny position* and *well-drained soil.* (You can tell whether your soil is adequately drained by digging several holes 0.80 m (about 2 ft 6 in) deep and noting whether these stay filled with water after a period of heavy rain.) If the natural drainage is not sufficient to prevent waterlogging, you can deal with the problem in one of two ways. The simplest method is to dig a trench about 0.80 m (2 ft 6 in) deep, put in a layer of rubble up to 30 cm (1 ft) deep, cover with a layer of turf and fill with soil to surface level. (**1**, left).

Alternatively, lay a system of land-drain pipes in trenches say 0.50 m (around 18 in) deep leading to a main drain and in turn to a soakaway situated at the lowest part of your plot (**1**, right).

Your vegetables need *soil that has been dug deep enough* to remove the roots of perennial weeds. They will need *light, sun and air.* Avoid windtunnels and draughty corners, which they hate. Surround and interlace your crops with *hard paths,* if only for the sake of your shoes and wheelbarrow. Whether your path is to be brick, cement or whatever it must have a good foundation of rubble or clinkers; this must be well rammed ('tamped') down (**2**). For a brick or paved path, lay a layer of mortar on the foundation and embed each brick or paving stone firmly into this. For a concrete path, lay the concrete about 8 cm (3 in) thick and form the edges with planks supported on their sides (**3**).

Have *water* close by – a standpipe, waterbutt or hosepipe. Keep crops clear of trees, hedges, shrubs. They rob the soil of plant foods and cast shade on growing plants. A wall or wood fence on the north side will protect crops from cold winds without impoverishing the soil or casting much shade. Reserve an out of the way corner for a garden shed connecting with a hard path. Keep a generous, shady spot for two compost heaps (see Natural and Artificial Aids), one on the boil, the other getting up steam. A south-facing, open spot is needed for a cold frame.

Remember that good cultivation from the start is all-important. You waste time and money if seeds fail to become plants, or plants get so strangled by weeds (**4**) they are too weak to produce a crop and are merely expensive compost-fodder.

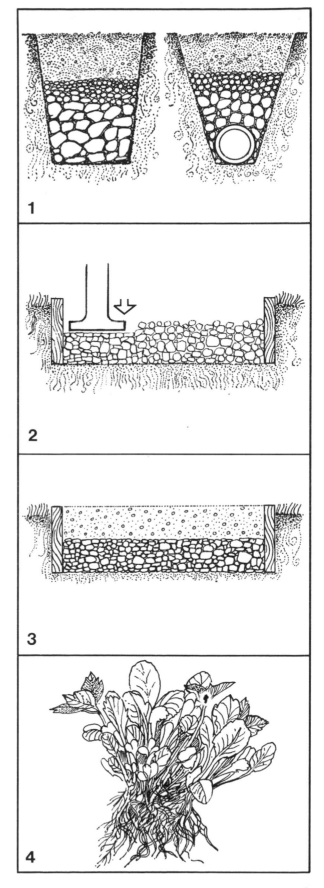

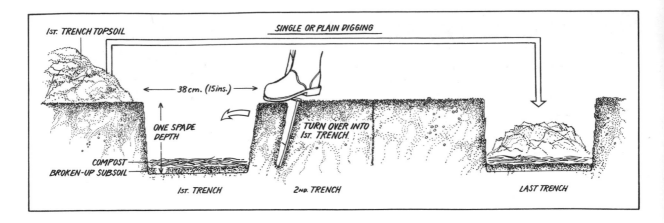

Figure labels: 1ST. TRENCH TOPSOIL — SINGLE OR PLAIN DIGGING — 38 cm. (15ins.) — ONE SPADE DEPTH — TURN OVER INTO 1ST. TRENCH — COMPOST — BROKEN-UP SUBSOIL — 1ST. TRENCH — 2ND. TRENCH — LAST TRENCH

WHEN TO START

Autumn is the best time to bring the soil into condition. Continuous frost, snow, rain and wind shatters the clods to a fine crumbly texture ('tilth') with no further effort. Backbreaking clay benefits most from this treatment; light, sandy soils gain nothing from being weathered and are sometimes beaten flat and solid by heavy winter rain. These can be dealt with in February or March, a few weeks before you start sowing and planting. Most vegetables grow easily without deep digging so long as the topsoil is fertile and the subsoil not a bog.

SINGLE OR PLAIN DIGGING

An initial digging is essential to get rid of perennial weeds which would lap up the food and moisture intended for the vegetables, and to improve the condition of the soil with compost or peat. Annual weeds can be killed with paraquat preparations such as WEEDOL, following the manufacturer's instructions strictly and *keeping it well out of the way of children;* alternatively, weeds can be chopped off with a hoe (see page 49). Rake the debris from the surface, then start digging.

Make a trench along the edge of the plot to the depth of the spade's blade. (The dug-out soil can be put in a barrow and used to fill in the last trench, or thrown onto the ground behind and gradually incorporated.) Remove all deep-rooted weeds, chop up the subsoil in the case of 'heavy' soil, and scatter compost or peat at the bottom. Start another row, turning the spadeful of earth upside down into the empty first trench, leaving it in rough clods. Continue in the same way until you have worked across your plot (see above).

Large, previously uncultivated plots can easily be prepared with a rotary cultivator (hire one or employ a gardening contractor). The organic matter is spread well over the surface and gets incorporated. Beware of rotovating ground which has not been cleared of such horrors as nettles, couchgrass and bindweed. These will be chopped into a multitude of potential offspring. Those on the surface will die but the buried bits can each turn into individual plants.

In subsequent years light soils need no digging at all apart from what is involved in harvesting the crops. Spread mulches – layers of old compost, peat, decayed manure, used hops, anything which does not contain viable weed seeds – to a depth of about 7–10 cm (3–4 in) and leave the rest to the worms and bacterial activity. (Mulching, see page 50.)

ROTATION

Though not absolutely essential, it is better for both crops and soil if they are shifted about so that they are not in the same place two years running. This prevents the soil from becoming exhausted and encouraging a permanent occupation by pests and diseases.

THE THREE YEAR PLAN

Whether the vegetable garden is small or large, it is possible to work on a three year plan. One part, **A**, for winter greens – broccoli, cabbage, sprouts, cauliflower, kales. Salad crops can also grow in the plot. A second part, **B**, is for root crops which split or 'fang' when the soil is too rich – beetroots, carrots, parsnips, swedes. They need ground which was manured a year previously. The third plot, **C**, is for peas, beans, onions, tomatoes, celery, spinach, in rich, freshly manured soil. Salads can also be grown among these.

In succeeding years the suggested crops play musical chairs, and get the best out of what each previous crop has left behind (see plan opposite).

This plan need not be stuck to rigidly. Much depends on what you choose to grow. Quick-growing summer salad crops, for instance, can be grown anywhere that is convenient at the time. Potatoes can be grown beside root crops, or almost anywhere provided the drainage is good. But for really heavy crops they need ground which was well-manured or compost-fed for a previous crop.

It's a good idea to sow dwarf second early peas among early potatoes. They stay warm and comfortable and grow fast, near the surface between the earthed-up rows, and need no stakes.

THREE YEAR ROTATION PLAN

1ST. YEAR

	A	B	C
	WINTER GREENS SALADS	ROOTS	PEAS BEANS ONIONS TOMATOES CELERY SPINACH
ADD	FERTILISER LIME	FERTILISER	COMPOST DUNG

2ND. YEAR

	B	C	A
	ROOTS	PEAS BEANS ETC.	WINTER GREENS SALADS
ADD	FERTILISER	COMPOST DUNG	FERTILISER LIME

3RD. YEAR

	C	A	B
	PEAS BEANS ETC.	WINTER GREENS SALADS	ROOTS
ADD	COMPOST DUNG	FERTILISER LIME	FERTILISER

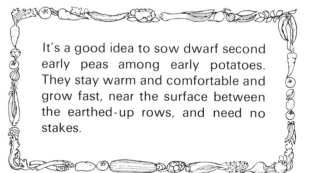

11

In a really small garden, true crop rotation is not practicable, or actually necessary, if the soil is well dug and fed annually (see page 48) with well rotted manure or compost. Just remember the general rule of moving crops around and knowing in advance where they are going to be, so that the ground can be given the appropriate diet. Vegetables, with the exception of permanent crops like globe artichokes and asparagus, are like gipsies and need to keep on the move. Winter greens, for instance, are likely to suffer from 'club root' (see opposite) if grown in the same ground for many years although the disease is less troublesome if the soil is well limed the previous year (see page 49).

THE TWO YEAR PLAN
If you cannot spare space for potatoes, have a two-year rotation: one group mainly of brassicas (winter greens), the other a mixture of anything you fancy.

Try to plan crops so that dwarf and tall are interspersed (see below, right), enabling light and air to reach them all without having to filter through forests of leaves. Never trust memory. Keep a record of what went where, and when, each year. Once a crop is cleared, it's forgotten.

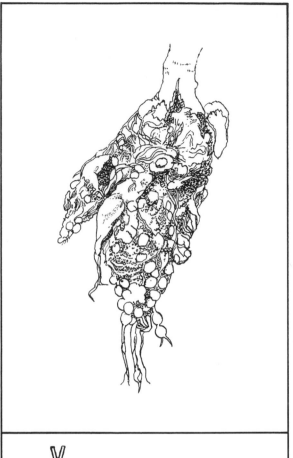

For convenience, the word 'brassica' is popularly used to include members of the cabbage family, such as Brussels sprouts, cauliflower, kale and broccoli (although the botanist groups a number of dissimilar-seeming vegetables such as turnip, radish and even mustard under this umbrella). Because they take so long to mature, most brassicas are sown in a seedbed and later transplanted.

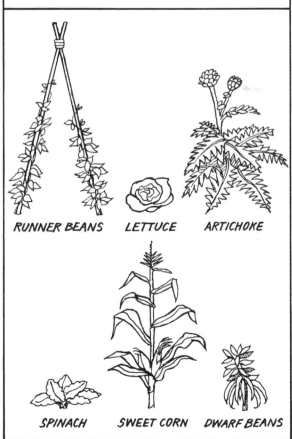

RUNNER BEANS   LETTUCE   ARTICHOKE

SPINACH   SWEET CORN   DWARF BEANS

INTERCROPPING

This method of cultivation involves growing crops of one type close to those of another which take longer to mature, eg, radish, summer spinach, lettuce, between rows of peas, (**1**), or salad crops between potato rows. They can be used young, leaving the main crop to grow on and mature. The rows should run from north to south so that the shorter plants are not shaded by the taller ones throughout the day.

SUCCESSIONAL CROPPING

This means sowing short rows of fast-growing salad crops at successive intervals throughout summer, in any available spaces (**2**). This prevents a glut and keeps up a continuous supply.

CATCH CROPPING

This means raising fast-maturing crops on ground intended for something else. Radishes can be sown in April where outdoor tomatoes are later to be planted, and lettuce where celery and winter brassicas (greens) will go (**3**). Chinese cabbage will grow in the space vacated by early potatoes. Ground used continuously and intensively in this way must be kept well nourished and watered.

SOWING

PREPARING THE GROUND

When the soil is dry enough in spring not to stick to the feet, rake or hoe it down to the depth of about 5–8 cm (2–3 in) and allow it to dry until it will crumble into fine particles. This may take several rakings and dryings depending on your soil. Firm the surface by treading all over it closely (**4**). Then rake again to provide a fine tilth, remove large stones and any remaining rough clods.

If you want to combine flowers and vegetables, remember that successions of radishes, lettuces and early carrots can be used to form attractive edging plants in a flowerbed.

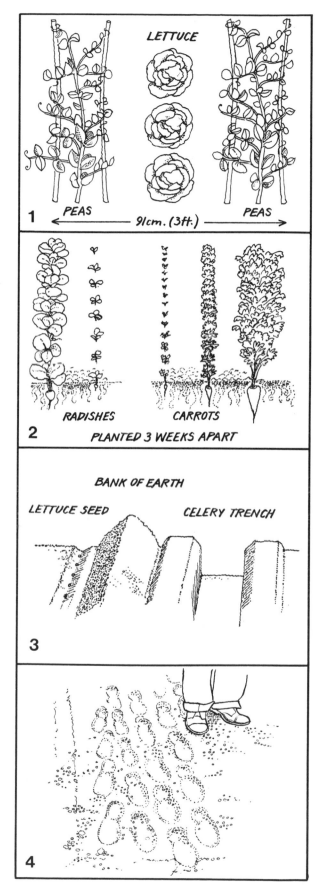

1 PEAS — LETTUCE — 91cm. (3ft.) — PEAS

2 RADISHES — CARROTS — PLANTED 3 WEEKS APART

3 BANK OF EARTH — LETTUCE SEED — CELERY TRENCH

4

Apart from perennials like asparagus and globe artichokes, vegetables fall roughly into two types. **a**: Those raised in a seedbed and transplanted when they are large enough to their permanent growing places with the least possible root disturbance (this group includes the cabbage family). **b**: Those which grow better undisturbed and are sown directly into drills the appropriate distance apart where they are to mature; they are thinned out at intervals to let each develop without overcrowding (most root vegetables, spinach and salads). Preparation of the soil for both nursery bed and main plot are the same, but the tilth need not be so fine for the larger seeds as for the tiny ones.

MAKING THE DRILLS
Mark out the positions of the rows with sticks, running north to south if possible; where strong winds are a problem, they can run from north-east to south-west. Stretch a line along each in turn and make the drills (**1**). Drills of about 1 cm ($\frac{1}{2}$ in) can be made by pressing a long bamboo cane on the surface beside the marker line and gently pressing it till it is just submerged (**2**). Another way to make a shallow drill is to draw a short stick along the ground beside the line (**3**). A broader drill can be made by pressing down the handle of the hoe or rake. The usual method is to use the edge of a hoe (**4**). In very dry weather the drills should be watered before the seed is sown.

One of the most common mistakes is to sow seed too deep and too thick. This results in poor germination and sickly seedlings. Most seeds should not be planted deeper than just over 1 cm ($\frac{1}{2}$ in); the exceptions are peas, beans, marrows, corn etc. A rough guide is that the drill should be three times as deep as the width of the seed.

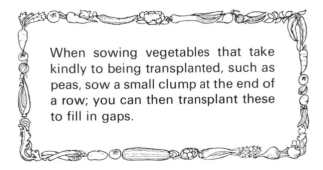

When sowing vegetables that take kindly to being transplanted, such as peas, sow a small clump at the end of a row; you can then transplant these to fill in gaps.

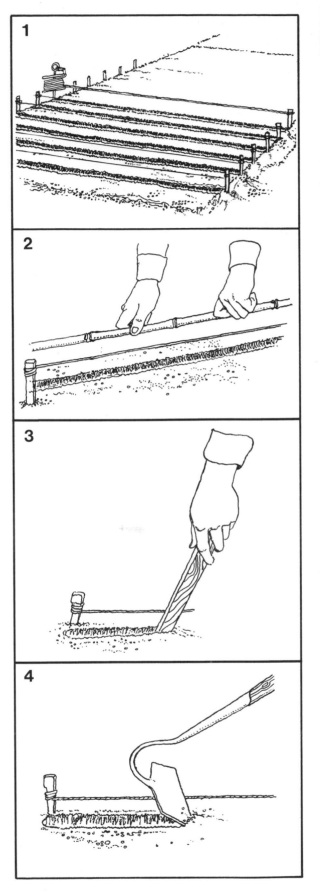

14

Sow the seeds thinly and evenly and close the drills with the back of a rake or by shuffling back the soil with the feet. The whole area which has been sown is afterwards lightly raked (**1**) to leave an even, porous surface through which rain can seep without 'puddling'.

THINNING

Thin the seedlings early (**2**), as soon as they can be handled, but do it in successive stages in case there are any failures in germination. Firm the ground around remaining seedlings.

PELLETED SEED

Many seeds are now sold in pelleted form. Each seed is given a coating of plant food. This protects them from disease while awaiting germination, which may be delayed by cold weather. It also gives the seedlings an additional boost as they start to grow. They are easier to handle as their jacket makes them larger than ordinary seed, and can be sown singly at the required distances. This saves considerable time in thinning and transplanting, and there is no wasted seed. The drills must be well watered if the soil is dry as the moisture helps to break down the food coating and assists germination.

TRANSPLANTING

Crops grown in a nursery bed such as leeks and brassicas are sown in short rows about 15 cm (6 in) apart. Thin them early and leave 2–3 cm (about 1 in) apart. The night before the seedlings are to be transplanted to their cropping positions, soak the bed thoroughly. This should be done before the plants become hard or lanky, but have a good root system. Lift only a few at a time so they don't dry out before they are back in the soil. Plant them out with a trowel or dibber (**3**, **4**), making plenty of room for the roots. Firm them in to leave no air pockets and give the plants a thorough watering.

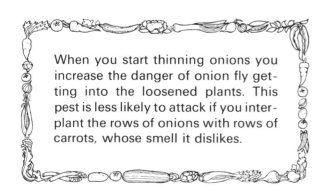

When you start thinning onions you increase the danger of onion fly getting into the loosened plants. This pest is less likely to attack if you interplant the rows of onions with rows of carrots, whose smell it dislikes.

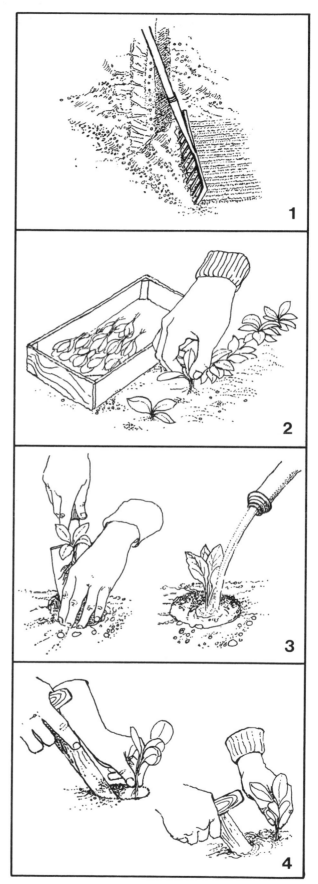

APPROXIMATE SOWING, PLANTING AND CROPPING TIMES

Vegetables	Sow	Set Out Plants	Final Plant Spacing	Space Between Rows	Cropping Time
Artichoke, Globe	—	March to May	1 to 1.20m (3-4 ft)	1m (3 ft)	June to July
Artichoke, Jerusalem	—	February to April	30cm (1 ft)	1m (3 ft)	November to February
Asparagus	—	February to March	45 cm (1 ft 6 in)	As convenient	May to June
Beans, broad	November to March	—	15 cm (6 in)	30 cm (1 ft)	June to July
Beans, dwarf	May to June	—	20 cm (8 in)	30 cm (1 ft)	July to September
Beans, runner and climbing	May to June	—	20 cm (8 in)	30 cm (1 ft)	August to October
Beetroot	April to June	—	15-20 cm (6 to 8 in)	30 to 40 cm (1 ft-1 ft 3 in)	July to October
Broccoli, heading	March to April	July	0.60 m (2 ft)	0.60 m (2 ft)	September to February
Broccoli, sprouting	May	July	0.75 m (2 ft 6 in)	0.75 m (2 ft 6 in)	January to April
Brussels sprouts	March to April	May	0.60 m (2 ft)	0.60 m (2 ft)	September to March
Cabbage, Savoy	March to May	July to August	0.60 m (2 ft)	0.60 m (2 ft)	November to Spring
Cabbage, Spring	July to September	September to October	40 cm (1 ft 4 in)	40 cm (1 ft 4 in)	March to May
Cabbage, Summer	March to April	—	22 cm (9 in)	30 cm (1 ft)	June onwards
Cabbage, Winter	March to May	—	50 cm (1 ft 8 in)	0.60 m (2 ft)	September to December
Cabbage, Chinese	May to June	July	20 cm (8 in)	30 cm (1 ft)	September to October
Carrot	March to July	—	5 cm (2 in)	20 cm (8 in)	June onwards

Vegetables	Sow	Set Out Plants	Final Plant Spacing	Space Between Rows	Cropping Time
Cauliflower, early	August to September	October	50 cm (1 ft 8 in)	0.60 m (2 ft)	May to June
Cauliflower, late	March	April	0.60 m (2 ft)	0.60 m (2 ft)	August
Celery (1) trenched	March to April	May to June	30 cm (1 ft)	30 cm (1 ft)	October onwards
Celery (2) Self-blanching	March to April	May to June	20 cm (8 in)	Plant in blocks	October onwards
Celeriac	As celery				
Cucumber, ridge	May	June	1m (3 ft)	1 m (3 ft)	July to September
Curly kale	April to June	July to August	60 cm (2 ft)	60 cm (2 ft)	Winter to early Spring
Kohlrabi	April to August	May to June	20 cm (8 in)	40 cm (1 ft 4 in)	August to January
Leek	March	May to June	20 cm (8 in)	15 cm (6 in)	November to March
Lettuce	March to June (September for Winter)	—	25-30 cm (9-12 in)	25-30 cm (9-12 in)	Continuous
Marrow	March to April	May to June	1-2 m (3-6 ft)	Space according to type	July to October
Onion	March to April	—	15 cm (6 in)	30 cm (1 ft)	April (for salads) to October (for storage)
Parsnip	March	—	20 cm (8 in)	45 cm (1 ft 6 in)	November onwards
Pea, early	November	—	8 cm (3 in)	45 cm (1 ft 6 in)	June
Pea, midseason	March	—	8 cm (3 in)	0.75 m (2 ft 6 in)	July
Pea, late	April to May	—	8 cm (3 in)	1m (3 ft)	September

Vegetables	Sow	Set Out Plants	Final Plant Spacing	Space Between Rows	Cropping Time
Potato, early	March to May	—	24 cm (10 in)	0.60 m (2 ft)	June to August
Radish	April onwards	—	—	15 cm (6 in)	Continuous
Salsify	April to May	—	20 cm (8 in)	30 cm (1 ft)	August onwards
Savoy: see Cabbage					
Seakale beet	April to June	—	30-40 cm (1 ft-1 ft 4 in)	30 cm (1 ft)	July onwards
Shallots	—	February to March	15-25 cm (6-10 in)	30 cm (1 ft)	July onwards
Spinach, summer	February to July	—	15 cm (6 in)	30 cm (1 ft)	June to September
Spinach, winter	August to September	—	15 cm (6 in)	30 cm (1 ft)	April to May
Spinach Beet	April to May (August for Spring)	—	30 cm (1 ft)	30 cm (1 ft)	August (and Spring)
Sweet Corn	May to June	—	40 cm (1 ft 4 in) (Plant in blocks, not single rows)	40 cm (1 ft 4 in)	August to September
Tomato, bush outdoors	March to early April	June	1-1.20m (3 ft-4 ft)	1-1.20m (3 ft-4 ft)	August to September
Tomato, dwarf, outdoors	March to early April	June	0.60 m (2 ft)	0.60 m (2 ft)	August to September
Turnip	March to September	—	20 cm (8 in)	40 cm (1 ft 4 in)	August onwards

Note As indicated in the heading to this section, the dates given are approximate only and will of course vary according to region and individual weather conditions.

Everyday Vegetables

Here are notes on the individual treatment needed for growing your 'mainstay' vegetables. Information about sowing times etc. is also given in the chart on pages 16–18.

BEANS

BROAD BEAN

The hardiest and most easily grown of the bean family (**1**). There are three sorts: longpods, the hardiest and best for sowing in autumn and spring; Windsors, best flavour; and the dwarf varieties. In some areas and soils the longpods can be sown in November and will stand the winter to provide an extra early crop. This is a waste of time and seed on heavy soil, as they will probably rot.

In spring and summer the maincrop will grow on both light and heavy land which has been well worked and manured for a previous crop. Make a drill 15 cm (6 in) wide and 5 cm (2 in) deep. Sow the beans in a double row, staggered so that they are 10–15 cm (4–6 in) apart 30 cm (1 ft) between each row (**2**). It doesn't matter which way up the seed is placed. Put a group of extra seeds at the end of each row as replacements for any losses. These can be transplanted later by trowel with a good ball of soil.

As soon as baby beans start forming from the bottom truss of flowers, pinch out the growing tips . . . about 8 cm (3 in) of the tender top and side shoots (**3**). This discourages blackfly – a continual problem with this crop – they don't like the taste of the older, tougher parts of the plant and cannot get established. The tips, treated as summer spinach, also provide one of the most delectable early vegetable dishes (see page 61).

The fully formed pods grow to a length of 15–30 cm (6–12in). Baby pods can be picked before the beans are properly formed and cooked whole (**4**); always pick them young before they go starchy and have a black eye. Pick often so that more will form. When the crop is over, cut off the tops and leave the roots to provide valuable nitrogen to the soil (this applies both to pea and bean crops). If the ground is needed for another crop at once, dig out the roots and put on the compost heap.

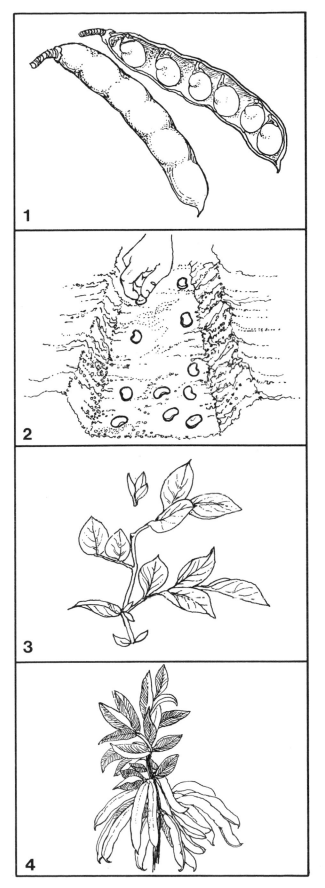

FRENCH BEAN

There are two types, the dwarf and the climbing. Each has good and bad points. The low ones are backbreakers to pick, though in dry weather you can straddle them on hands and knees, if food is of more importance than dignity. In wet weather the pods are beaten to the ground and get dirty, and rot if not rescued. Newer varieties (**1**) hold their beans above their leaves and avoid this nuisance. No stakes needed. The climbers are more difficult to place. They have a longer cropping period, but need support, and cast shade.

Dwarf French: suitable for the smallest garden, pots or even windowboxes. They can be sown in double or single rows, the seeds 20 cm (8 in) apart. Water well in dry weather so the pods do not get hard and stringy. Pick the young beans regularly and carefully. A careless tug can leave you with the uprooted plant in your hand.

Climbing French: may be grown against a fence, round poles (**2**), as a hedge, or up trellis or netting (**3**) against a sunny wall. Sown and crops earlier than the runner bean, and combines the distinctive flavour of dwarf French varieties with the heavy cropping of runner beans. Sow the seeds thinly 2–3 cm (1 in) deep from late April to early June. They like a warm soil best, can tolerate a cool one, and object strongly to a wet one. Nip out the growing point when the plants are 15 cm (6 in) tall, so they will produce side shoots and become bushy. Stop them growing beyond their supports. Give frequent waterings during a dry season, and a mulch during warm weather to conserve moisture.

RUNNER BEAN

Rich soil, sow from May till late June, 5 cm (2 in) deep, 20 cm (8 in) apart, with 30 cm (1 ft) between rows. Give the same kind of support (**4**) and treatment as climbing beans, but sow two weeks later.

BEETROOT

Beetroot is a maritime plant which likes sandy and salty conditions. Give a dressing of common salt in July, 20 g per m² (½ oz per sq yd), during a showery spell. It is also a dual-purpose plant. Take a few leaves at a time from each of the young plants and cook as spinach. Or the whole top can be used of those pulled as thinnings. The leaves of golden beet have the best flavour, superior to summer spinach. The roots of the white beet have

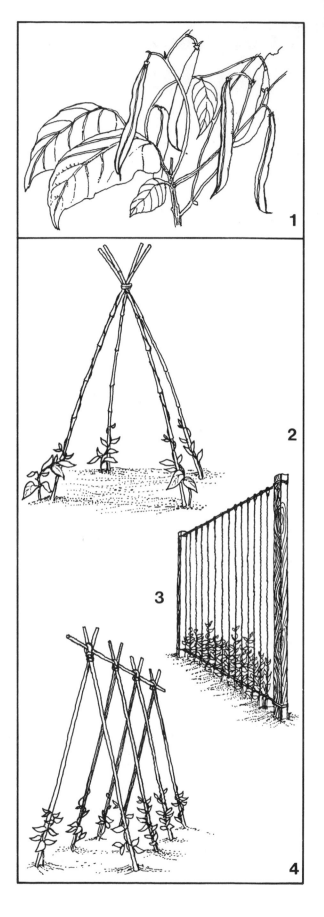

the sweetest and most subtle flavour. Lift the crop in October before frost, and store for winter use. See Storing.

There are several types (**1**) — round or globe; long; red; golden or white. Red, globe varieties are the most popular. Sow in drills 2–3 cm (1 in) deep in light soil, from April till June. Keep the soil moist all the time or the roots will become coarse and woody. When the roots are still quite small, pull up alternate ones and use as hot vegetable, or in salads, or pickle them, to leave room for the remainder to develop (**2**).

BROCCOLI

LARGE HEADING
These produce dense curds protected by self-folding leaves (**3**). This type is hardy, sown in March and April and ready for use in autumn and winter; though by planting several varieties you can have them maturing almost throughout a gentle year. Sow outdoors in March and April, 2–3 cm (1 in) deep in a seedbed or 'broadcast' and transplant when about 10 cm (4 in) tall, spacing plants about 60 cm (2 ft) apart, with the same distance between rows.

SPROUTING, PURPLE AND WHITE
Extremely hardy and provides a succession of shoots from early spring till midsummer (**4**). It is tall and needs protection from wind so the roots are not rocked. Some varieties, Nine Star, can remain for several years. Most are sown in May.

BRUSSELS SPROUTS
These are grown in the same way as broccoli, but need a longer growing time, as they crop continuously from September to the end of March. To get firm rock-hard sprouts, they need a well-manured soil and very firm planting. Loose soil produces loose sprouts. Sow the seed not later than April in drills about 2–3 cm ($\frac{1}{2}$ in) deep. In autumn remove any yellowing leaves to the compost heap, or on heavy, sticky ground, lay them as a 'path' between the rows.

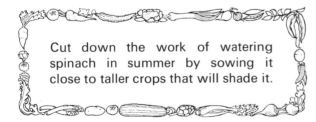

Cut down the work of watering spinach in summer by sowing it close to taller crops that will shade it.

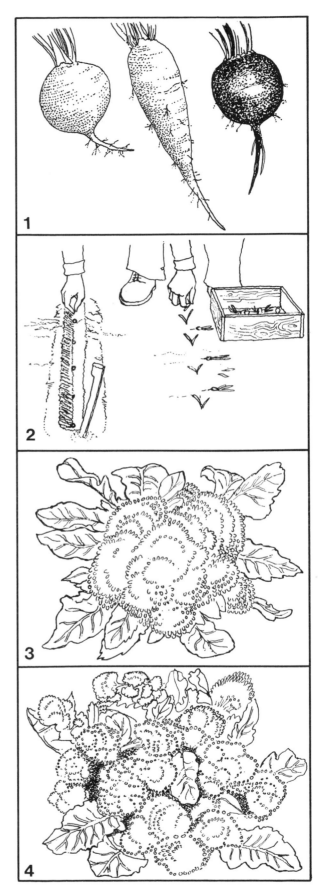

Always make a point of picking your sprouts from the bottom up, a few at a time from each plant (**1**). The tops can be used as 'cabbages' after winter and when the weather warms up in spring; the remaining sprouts will 'shoot' and provide a most delectable dish. Before they start to flower, break off the shoots where they are still tender and boil them fast and briefly.

CABBAGE

There are several different kinds and shapes giving a choice of crops round the year: ballhead (**2**, right), with round hearts; pointed (**2**, top), with conical hearts; Savoy, with wrinkled leaves (**2**, left). There are quick summer growers, others which will stand the winter, and spring cabbage. Sow all types in a seedbed 2 cm ($\frac{3}{4}$ in) deep and transplant seedlings when about 15 cm (6 in) high. Plants should be 40 cm (16 in) apart with the same distance between rows. Sow in March–April for summer and autumn cropping and July-August for spring cropping. Quick-growing types can be sown thinly in rows and thinned out by using the leafy ones as a purée and leaving the rest to heart up.

CARROT

Many types but the earliest are the most delicious. Soil must be very fine and not freshly manured. Stump rooted varieties with candle shaped roots are the most generally useful (**3**); long carrots are mainly used for exhibition. Sow March–July. If sown thinly the small round kinds need little thinning, others can be thinned progressively till 5 cm (2 in) apart. Keep them growing quickly by watering if necessary. Use from June onwards. Splitting can be caused by heavy rain followed by drought, or by too rich soil. Their worst pest is carrot fly (see Pests).

CAULIFLOWER

Although it looks very like heading broccoli, it has a more delicate flavour and constitution; not as hardy. Cauliflower must be grown quickly in good, well-firmed and manured soil. A sunny, sheltered spot is best. The ground needs to be dug deeply and hoed regularly. Plants should be spaced about 50 cm (20 in) apart with 60 cm (2 ft) between rows. As the curds develop break some of the inner leaves over them to keep them white and protected from rain or frost (**4**).

22

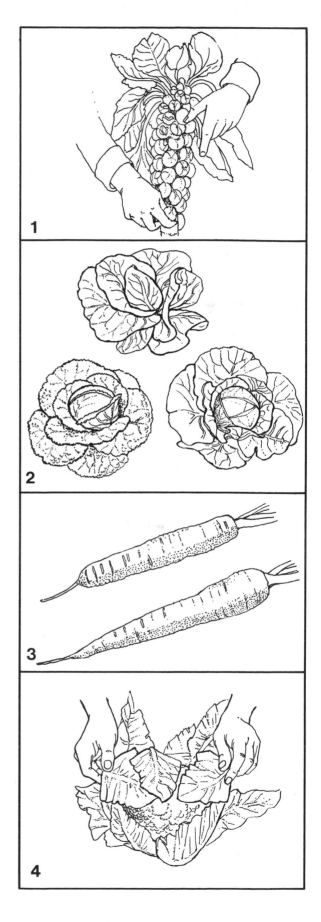

CELERY

Two kinds, self-blanching to use in late summer and autumn and the ordinary white or pink variety for winter use. This is crisp and tender only after hard frost and needs more attention than the self-blanching type. Buy the plants unless you have means of raising them in gentle heat. Seed must be sown March to April to have made good-sized plants to set out at the end of May or during June.

SELF-BLANCHING

This type needs no trenching. Grow it on the flat in well-manured soil which will retain moisture in summer. Set out plants about 20 cm (8 in) apart in blocks so they will blanch themselves by the leaves shading the stems (1). No earthing up is necessary.

NON-SELF-BLANCHING

This type needs to be grown in a well-enriched trench, 30 cm (1 ft) deep and wide enough to allow for a double row (2). Tread down the humus material, compost or manure, as firm planting is most important. Start to blanch the plants in late July when they are about 30 cm (1 ft) high. Remove any side shoots, then wrap newspaper around the stems and tie with raffia loosely enough to allow the hearts to develop. This keeps the stems clean as soil is gradually drawn up around the plants (3). A second earthing up is done at the end of August and again a month later while the soil is still workable. Full blanching should not be done till the plants have stopped growing, leaving only the top furl of leaves exposed. Keep them well fed and watered throughout their growing life. It is almost impossible to give them too much to drink.

Begin lifting at the end of the row, after a sharp frost, which ensures crispness. Scrape back some of the soil first so that the fork can go well into the ground without damaging the stems (4).

Dangers Celery fly lays eggs on the foliage in midsummer and the leaves blister and decay. These can be pinched to kill the maggots but a preventative spray is better in June and again three weeks later. Brown spots on the leaves indicate leaf spot and must be sprayed at once (see page 56).

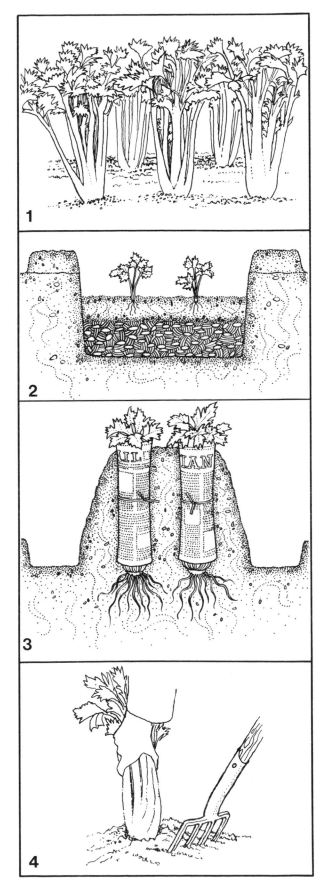

CUCUMBER, ridge

These are grown in the open. A good strain can be as good as a frame or greenhouse variety. Choose a sunny, open spot protected from strong winds. The seeds can be raised in pots in mid-April or put direct into the ground in mid-May; the plants need to be about 1 m (3 ft) apart. Soil must be rich, moist and well-drained (**1**). The plants can be trained up, down or sideways against any support you choose, to save space. They can be grown in pots in balconies, or trailed down a steep sunny bank.

Nip out the growing tips when 6–7 leaves have formed to encourage side shoots. Never let the plants lack moisture or the fruits will stop forming, but be careful not to wash away the soil and expose the roots. There is no need to remove female flowers (**2**) as is the case with frame cucumbers, since these need to be pollinated by pollen from the male flowers (**3**).

LEEK

One of the easiest and hardiest vegetables to grow. Hardly worth the trouble of raising your own seed as the young plants can be bought cheaply in June. They need soil which is rich and retains moisture but never becomes 'boggy'. Use a dibber to make holes 12 cm (5 in) deep and 15–22 cm (6–9 in) apart, depending on eventual thickness of variety. Leave about 15 cm (6 in) between each row. Drop down a plant into each hole so that only the leaf tops show above the rim, then water the holes thoroughly but do not fill with soil (**4**). Then leave alone till they are the size you want. They can be left in the ground over winter and dug as wanted, or lifted and bundled together in a trench 'heeled in' in a sheltered part of the garden. 'Heeling in' means providing a temporary home for plants which have been lifted, by covering them with soil which is then gently firmed with the heel.

LETTUCE

Sow in succession in a warm border at intervals of 3 weeks from March until the end of June. Needs moderately rich soil and plenty of moisture so that it will mature quickly. Can be transplanted from 25–30 cm (9–12 in) apart each way, according to variety.

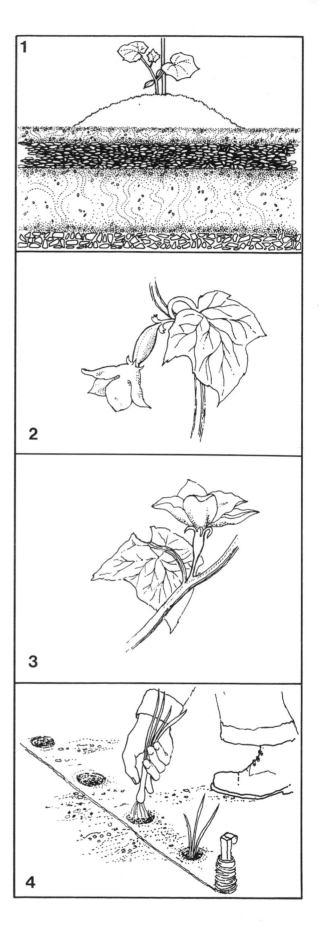

MARROW

Many different kinds, both bush (**1**) and trailing, some more suitable for winter storing than others. All need very rich, moisture-retaining soil. If there is not enough good manure or compost to dig into the whole bed, take out individual holes 30 cm (1 ft) deep and 0.60 m (2 ft) across, and fill these with rich, moist, humus material (**2**). Leave the surface slightly below ground level; in dry weather the plants can be flooded with water which will go directly to the roots, rather than spread across the topsoil.

The seeds can be grown indoors during March and April for planting outside in late May, or where they are to grow in the last two weeks of May. Put seeds on an edge rather than flat, to avoid rotting, and add a few extra ones at the end of the row to replace failures. Allow about 1 m (3 ft) apart for bush types and 1.50 m (5 ft) for trailers. These should have the tips of the main growth pinched out when they are about 1 m (3 ft) long. As with all trailers they can be grown up fences or poles. Keep 'courgette' types harvested regularly (**3**). If any are allowed to grow 'marrow' size the plant will stop producing new growth and flowers.

ONION

GROWING FROM SETS
Onion 'sets' are frustrated seedlings, grown so late in the season that there is no possibility of their putting on enough weight for kitchen use. These are bought by the pound and planted in March — April. Plant with a trowel or dibber and leave just the tips showing. Birds often pull out the sets, from mischief or to use the tops as bedding. Push the bulbs back but if there is a large attack, guard them with netting or black string.

GROWING FROM SEED
These need good and crumbly soil. They can be grown on the same ground year after year which is gradually improved with manure, peat, wood ashes, lime etc. Sow in March — April. Use the thinnings (**4**) for salads, and leave them 15 cm (6 in) apart for average sized varieties and 20 cm (8 in) for 'monsters'. Hoe regularly in summer, water freely when necessary and never let the soil dry out completely. If any flower heads start to form break or crush the stems.

When growth slows down in summer, bend over the tops, if this does not happen naturally, to

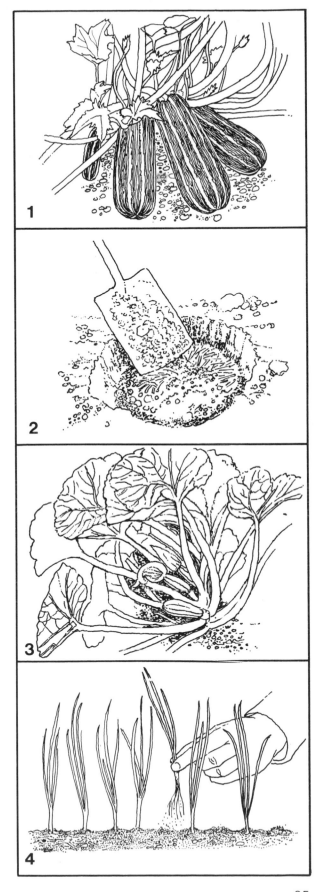

help ripening. Lift bulbs with a fork when fully developed and let them dry in the sun (**1**), preferably protected from rain, eg, a well-ventilated frame covered by glass or clear plastic. Tie in ropes and hang up to continue drying (**2**). (See also Storing.)

Troubles If leaves turn yellow and wilt, take action against eelworm and onion fly (see Pests). Sometimes they bolt (go to seed) before they are large enough to harvest. This is usually caused by sowing too early in the year. If cold weather checks growth, this sets the flowering process in motion.

PARSNIP

Less trouble to grow than carrots. The soil the same as for other root crops; well forked over for a previous crop, but not recently manured or the roots will fork. Be patient, the seeds may be slow to germinate. Sow 3–4 seeds together at 20 cm (8 in) intervals in drills 2–3 cm (1 in) deep and about $\frac{1}{2}$ m (18 in) apart (**3**). These are later singled, leaving the strongest plant at each position (**4**). Roots can be lifted from the end of October but have a better flavour if exposed to frost; they can be left in the ground throughout winter.

PEAS

These are listed by the seasons in which they crop, first early, second early, maincrop, late. There are dwarf, medium and tall varieties, with seeds round or wrinkled. The round ones are hardier and can be planted earlier, but have not the flavour of the wrinkled ones. Peas need rich soil containing plenty of chalk or lime, well dug for a previous crop and moisture-retentive; pea seeds will not germinate in a cold, wet soil.

Since parsnip seeds are so slow to germinate, it's a good idea to sow lettuce, which germinates and matures quickly, here and there between the clusters of parsnip seeds, to mark their position before the seedlings come up.

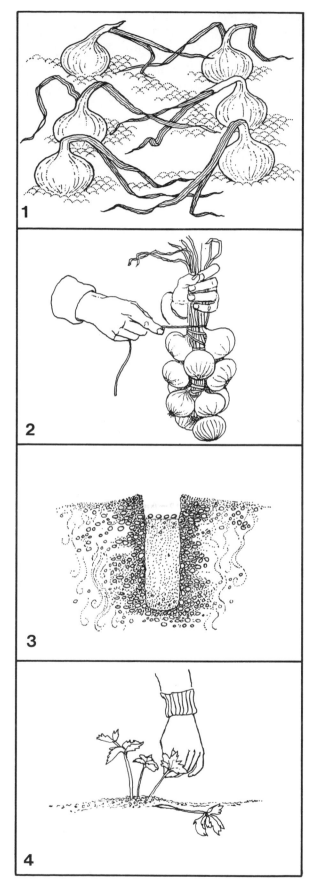

26

Sow in drills 5 cm (2 in) deep (**1**, left), or in trenches of 5 cm x 20 cm (8 in) wide. Space the seeds evenly 5–8 cm (2–3 in) apart. The space between the rows should be equal to the height of each variety. Protect seedling from birds (**1**, right).

Dwarf varieties will crop reasonably well without sticks, but are more prolific (and cleaner) if supported by hazel branches or one of the many forms of plastic netting available (**2**). Do not thin the seedlings, and be cautious handweeding between them so as not to avoid disturbing the tender and shallow pea roots by pulling up sizeable thistles, chickweed, etc. Better to snip off their tops and deal with the roots when the peas are over. Protect from birds and mice – mice, by traps after sowing; birds, from sowing to cropping.

POTATO, early

For the best yield start off the tubers by allowing them to sprout in a light, frostproof room. Egg trays are splendid for this, or shallow boxes (**3**). In January, stand them up, eye ends uppermost, until well sprouted (**4**, left). A large, well-sprouted tuber can be cut through the middle (**4**, centre); in a badly sprouted tuber, which has been allowed to go too far, the shoots are tall and straggly (**4**, right).

Once sprouted, plant them in trenches during March and April about 12 cm (5 in) deep, 23–25 cm (9–10 in) apart, in rows 0.60–1 m (2–3 ft) apart. Sprinkle a general fertiliser on the surface after planting. When shoots appear, draw a little soil from between the rows and over them. Continue this earthing up as the stems lengthen to keep the tubers from the light. If they become exposed and go green they are inedible. They will grow in almost any soil provided it is not water-logged.

RADISH

Before sowing, top dress with general fertiliser, as radishes need rich soil to grow quickly for good flavour and texture. Sow thinly in shallow drills set 15 cm (6 in) apart, fortnightly from April to August and water frequently in hot weather; they do best in a damp, shady situation. Alternatively they can be scattered into unwanted soil rather than grown in rows. (For top dressing, see page 48.)

Dangers Flea beetle is a common hazard (see Pests); protection from birds is advisable.

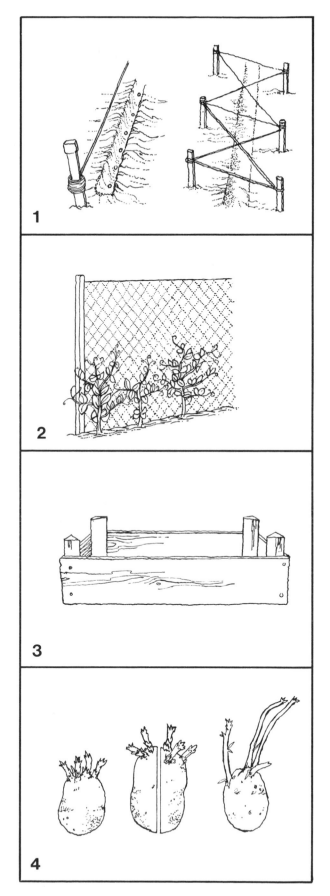

SHALLOTS

Grow as for onion sets, but the soil need not be so rich. They can be bought by weight early in the year. Press very firmly into the soil with the tips just showing in February and March 15–25 cm (6–10 in) apart in rows about 30 cm (1 ft) apart. Unlike onion sets which simply grow into one large onion, one shallot will form into a cluster of bulbs (**1**). Hoe between rows frequently and in June scrape some soil away from the clusters so that the light will help them to ripen. As soon as foliage dies down, lift the bulbs and lay them on the surface for a few days before storing in an airy cool frostproof place. They will keep for the best part of a year.

SPINACH

The two best-known kinds are usually described as round-seeded (summer) and prickle-seeded (winter). By growing both it is possible to have a supply throughout the year. It is a crop which needs to grow fast and will not behave in hot, dry conditions. Summer varieties are the worst for 'bolting'. Sow the seeds 2–3 cm (1 in) deep in drills set 30 cm (1 ft) apart. Sow summer spinach in small quantities once every two weeks from February to mid-July (up to a month or so later for winter varieties). When plants touch in the rows, snip out alternate ones for use and leave the rest to grow on. From these gather leaves as wanted (**2**).

SPINACH BEET

Known also as 'perpetual spinach', and does not bolt like the summer variety. Sow in April and August in drills 2–3 cm (1 in) deep and 30 cm (1 ft) apart. The later sowing will give a most useful early spring crop. Keep the leaves gathered to encourage a fresh supply (**3**)

TURNIP

This vegetable must grow quickly to be sweet and tender, rather than coarse and woody. Turnips need rich, moist soil. Sow in small quantities every few weeks from March to August. The seedbed should be firm and the drills very shallow. Thin to 15–23 cm (6–9 in). Pull them when they are young and tender, before they are the size of tennis balls (**4**).

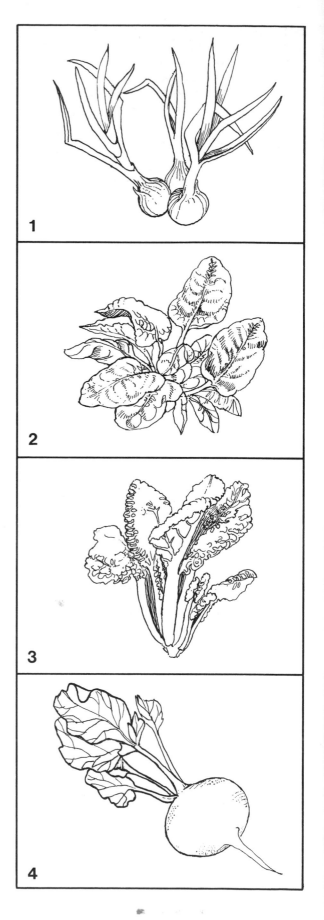

1

2

3

4

Crops for the Gourmet

Many unusual and delicious vegetables, thought to be luxuries and seldom found in local shops, are no more difficult to grow than the humble potato.

ARTICHOKE

GLOBE

An impressive, permanent plant frequently grown in flower borders for the beauty of the silvery leaves and stately stem, which grows 1.20–1.80 m high (4–6 ft). This is crowned with a large, handsome bud (**1**) with several smaller offspring on short side shoots below. If allowed to bloom rather than being cut for the pot when still tight-furled, the buds turn into large purple-blue thistle-like flowers, much in demand by flower arrangers. If you fail to catch it for the pot, you can still have it for the eye.

Buy young rooted plants ('offsets') from nurseries from March to May. Give them rich, deep, moist, well-drained soil preferably in the sun. They need armfuls of room, 1–1.20 m (3–4 ft) apart and around 1 m (3 ft) from the edge of a path, or you will be lashed by their leaves (**2**). Plant about 10 cm (4 in) deep.

Once the plants have settled in, you can multiply your stock endlessly by taking suckers, 'offsets' from the parent plants, after they have produced 3 or 4 crops. In April, clear the ground around the main plant, and with a sharp knife or spade slice off the outer growing sections with some root attached. Plant these as you would the bought 'offsets' and water well until they 'take'.

Spread manure, or your favourite fertiliser, around the plants every spring. Like so many silver-leaved plants, they are not reliably hardy and need some protection in the worst winter weather. This can be straw or ashes, over the crowns, but take it off early in spring before you create a mini-compost heap and rot the plants completely.

JERUSALEM

A hardy herbaceous perennial, with edible potato-like roots (**3**). The plants can stay in the same place for ten years or more; take them straight from the ground as you need them. They eventually become an underground matted entanglement,

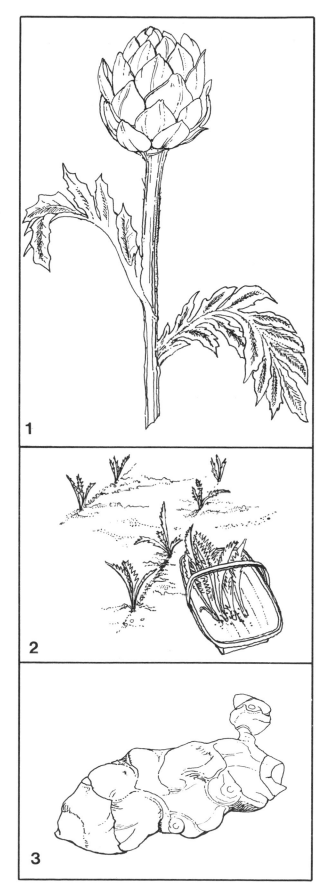

and the roots smaller, difficult both to dig out and scrub clean. For this reason dedicated eaters and growers replant every year. Artichokes are the easiest of all vegetables to grow, immune to most diseases and pests and willing to grow in any odd corner, though an open and sunny position will produce the largest tubers. Start with a good modern silver-skinned variety, vastly superior to the old knobbly one. Plant from February to April, 8–10 cm (3–4 in) deep and 30 cm (1 ft) apart in rows about 1 m (3 ft) apart. Choose the smoothest tubers from the previous crop, about the size of a large hen egg, for replanting a new bed.

Virtues and faults The plants grow from 2–$2\frac{1}{2}$ m (7–8 ft or so) which makes them a useful windbreak, or an unhelpful shadow on young growing crops which need full sun to ripen them.

ASPARAGUS

Don't be put off by out-of-date advice about raised beds and all kinds of hidden mysteries. All you need is to like it well enough to give up ground all the year for a crop lasting about two months . . . for the next 20 to 40 years! On the credit side, it needs very little attention.

You can grow from seed or buy one- or two-year-old plants. (Don't be tempted to buy three-year-olds in the hope that you can start cutting the shoots in the first year; their roots are too large and old to stand the transfer.) The seedlings should be out of the ground for the minimum of time when being transplanted; their roots must be kept moist under a sack or similar cover. As it is a permanent crop, the soil must be extra rich and well drained, particularly if it is to be grown on the flat rather than in a raised bed.

Dig a trench about 23 cm (9in) deep and wide. Keep a ridge of soil down the middle (**1**) on which the crowns (growing tips) can 'ride' with their long roots astride. Cover the crowns with 8 cm (3 in) of soil (**2**) and allow rather less than $\frac{1}{2}$ m (18 in) between the plants. Grow in double or single rows at a distance apart to suit yourself. Opinions vary. There are no rigid rules.

Start cutting when the plants are three years old (**3**). The most usual period is from early May to the middle of June. But if you plant a number of different varieties you can cheat considerably about this nicety. Leave the fern to return nourishment to the roots till it turns yellow, then cut it off at ground level (**4**).

30

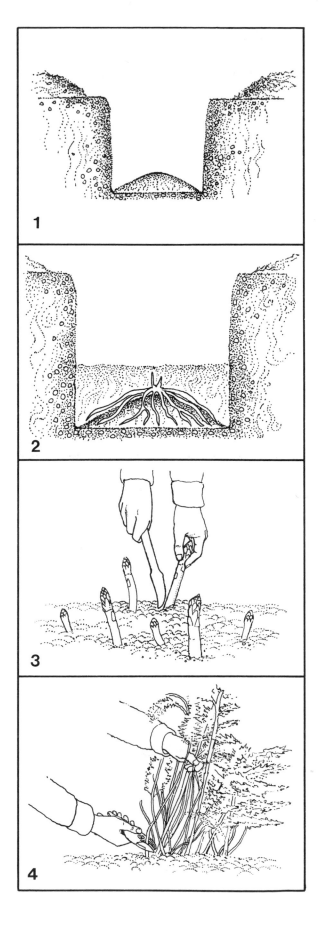

CHINESE CABBAGE

Not a true cabbage, despite its name. It belongs to the mustard group of the large brassica family, and is really more like a cos lettuce (**1**). The crisp, sweet heart can be eaten raw and the outer leaves cooked like cabbage. Sow in succession 20 cm (8 in) apart, with 30 cm (1 ft) between rows when the ground warms up, and keep well watered. They are not completely hardy and will bolt at the hint of frost or if the soil is allowed to dry out. Late May and June are the safest sowing times for any but mild districts. You can fit them between two rows of tall growing vegetables where the soil is shaded. Once the heads start to swell tie the leaves together with raffia or string to help them blanch. Use as soon as they are reasonably firm, about 9 weeks after sowing.

CELERIAC

Known in America as knob celery. It concentrates its energies on producing swollen roots rather than crisp stems (**2**).

Grow as celery but take care not to plant too deeply. The seedlings should be planted out in shallow drills, 30 cm (1 ft) apart (**3**). Give plenty of water and food. As the roots swell draw away the soil and remove the side shoots.

Vegetables are said to have 'bolted' when instead of producing leaves they run to seed; the most usual causes are that the soil is deficient in nitrogen, or that the weather has been too dry and they have not grown fast enough.

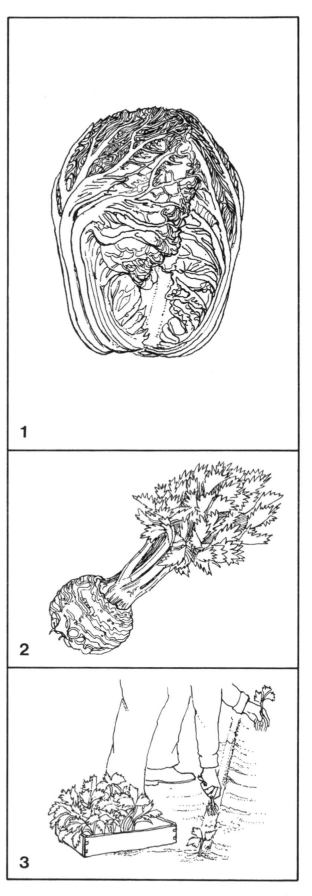

1

2

3

KOHLRABI

Despite the fact that it is listed in most seed catalogues, few people grow this rather peculiar-looking vegetable (**1**). Though used as a root crop, the green or purple 'roots' grow completely above the soil surface. Use them when no larger than a small orange, and for this purpose sow a small quantity at a time. They will grow much larger but be too tough and fibrous to enjoy. Often recommended as an alternative crop where conditions are too dry for turnips, it is far better than a substitute, milder and nuttier and as good raw as cooked.

Grow on good soil which has been matured for a previous crop. Sow in succession from end of April until August, thinly in drills 1 cm ($\frac{1}{2}$ in) deep in rows about 40 cm (16 in) apart. Thin the seedlings to leave 20 cm (8 in) between.

SALSIFY

Known as the 'vegetable oyster'. This is a loose, wishful reference to flavour, which does justice neither to oysters or salsify. It resembles a small parsnip, though with a finer texture and delicate taste. Sow in shallow drills in April and May. Thinnings can be used as small roots and later ones left at about 20 cm (8 in) apart. Ready for use from late summer, and can be left in the ground and lifted as wanted in winter (**2**).

SEAKALE BEET

A handsome plant with thick silver stalks and glossy spinach leaves: also called Swiss chard (**3**). Grow in the same way as spinach beet (see page 28). Break off both stem and leaf at the same time but serve separately. Cook the leaves as spinach and the mid-ribs in the same way as celery.

SWEET CORN

Give it a well manured, sunny spot, sheltered from strong winds which would rock the tall stems and loosen the shallow roots. The plants must grow in a block rather than single rows, so that pollen from the central flower falls on the lower and surrounding silky tassels to fertilise them, rather than blowing on to an adjoining row of unappreciative beans. Sow 2–3 cm (1 in) deep in early May; thin to about 40 cm (16 in) apart (**4**).

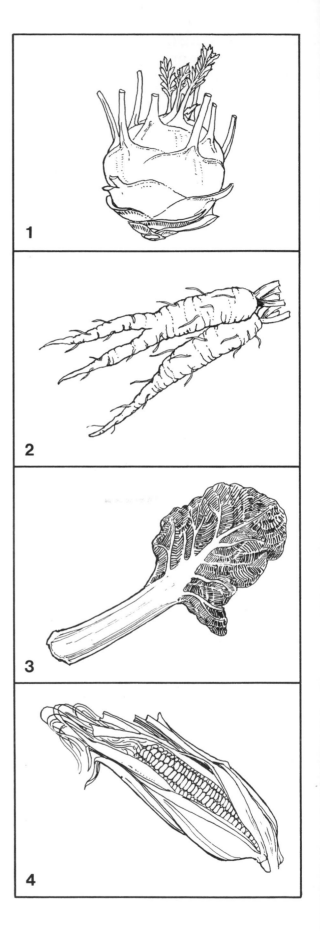

TOMATO, OUTDOORS

Seed is so cheap compared with the bought fruit, that it is worth taking a chance on a good summer with dwarf and bush varieties, which need little attention. Sow seed thinly in boxes or pots in March in any indoor place with a temperature of around 16°C (60°F). Gradually harden off the seedlings by putting them outside on 'friendly' days. Plant outdoors in a rich, well-drained, sunny place towards the end of May, depending on local conditions. Bush varieties spread sideways and need about 1–1.20 m (3–4 ft) all round. The dwarfs need about 50–60 cm (1½–2 ft). They should be left to grow naturally, needing no staking, no pinching, and very little attention, apart from a layer of straw or litter around the base of the plants to keep the fruit off the soil. Break off the growing tips if the plants are getting out of hand.

Single-stemmed varieties need to be supported firmly by stakes (**1**) and to have the side shoots which grow in the axils of the leaves with the main stem removed (**2**). As soon as the plant has produced four flower trusses, pinch out the main growing point. Water freely, particularly in warm weather.

Ring culture In cases where soil is precious, this method (**3**) is useful for growing single-stemmed varieties out of doors, although it is normally used for greenhouse cultivation. When the plants have reached the planting out stage, they are placed in special bottomless rings filled with John Innes No 3 compost or alternatively a special tomato compost. The rings are then stood on a 15 cm (6 in) layer of sterile pea gravel, ashes or sand. The latter is kept constantly moist while the compost in the rings is fed weekly with a liquid fertiliser when the fruit has formed. Two root systems develop, feeding roots in the compost and 'drinking' roots in the aggregate.

Even if you have only a balcony or other tiny space available you can still grow tomatoes, using the ready prepared polythene bags filled with a proprietary compost obtainable from gardening centres; directions are supplied with the bag.

Take great care when using hormone weedkiller sprays near tomato plants. The leaves may show a yellow mottle and slight crinkling, and the tomatoes may be misshapen and hollow.

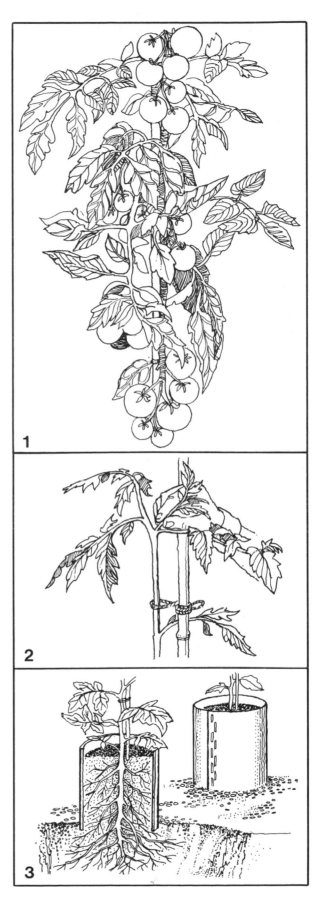

1

2

3

SUGGESTED VARIETIES FOR FINEST FLAVOUR

BEAN, BROAD
Dreadnought: well-filled, longpod variety.
Dwarf, The Midget: extremely high yield for small gardens. Needs no stakes. 30–38 cm (12–15 in) high, 45 cm (18 in) across.
Promotion: robust plants 0.90–1.20 m (3–4 ft) high. An abundance of pods 20–25 cm (8–10 in) long. High yield and packed with flavour.
Red Epicure: the finest flavour of all, but not for those who want electric green colouring. The pods are green, the inner beans, crimson. When cooked they turn to a deep straw colour. Hardy, and vigorous.

BEAN, DWARF, FRENCH
Glamis: specially bred for rugged and outlandish positions with the nastiest weather extremes.
Pencil Pod Black Wax (Golden Butter): round, tender, fleshy, 15 cm (6 in) high; slightly curved pods.
Remus: long, narrow, absolutely stringless pods above the foliage, so flowers fertilise more quickly and pods are kept clear of the ground and rain splashes. Can be eaten raw or fully mature.

BEAN, RUNNER AND CLIMBING FRENCH
Romano: stringless and snaps easily. Outstanding flavour.
Violet Podded Stringless: delightful deep purple-blue when growing, turning to rich green after 2 minutes in boiling water. Heavy cropper and easy to manage.
White Stringless Fry (Dobies): Long, smooth slender. Heavy pickings from July to August.

BEETROOT
Boltardy: unlike many varieties, will not take to its heels and bolt from an early sowing. Deep red, sweet fresh flavour and no hint of fibre even from elderly roots.
Snowhite: ice white and far exceeding the flavour of the red varieties. Serve hot or cold, in salads or with fish or meat. The wavy leaf is high in vitamins; cook as spinach.

BROCCOLI
Early White: more delicate flavour than Early Purple.
Nine Star Perennial: each spring produces a large central head surrounded by 8 or 9 smaller heads. Use all before they go to seed and the plants will yield for several years on well manured ground.

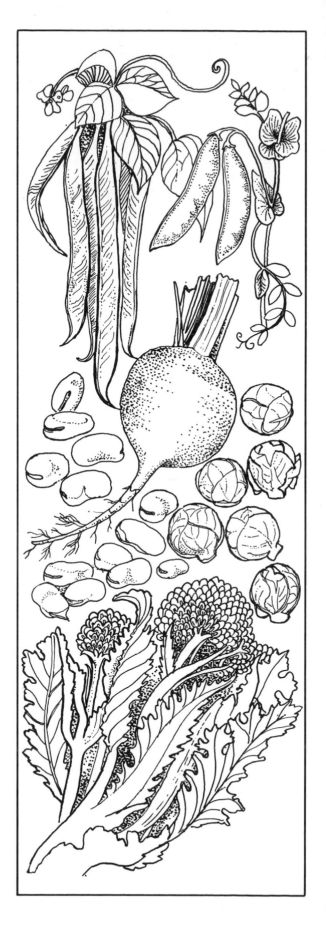

BRUSSELS SPROUTS

Focus: a distinctive savoury flavour. The sprouts are small, dark and firm, mature from September to January, and remain on the stem in tip-top form and flavour without splitting or blowing.

F1 Hybrid Fasholt: the finest late variety. Medium sized sprouts reaching their peak in the first half of January and remaining firm for use during most of February.

Noisette: a dwarf type producing tight, firm little buttons which need no trimming and have a superb, nutty flavour. Only a 'Master' Worst Cook could make them watery.

Prince Astrol: late variety, tightly packed.

CARROT

Little Finger: early, slender, almost coreless and delicious. Short and sweet. A tubby, 7–10 cm (3–4 in) long variety with extra sweet flavour which grows well in both light and heavy soil.

CUCUMBER, RIDGE

Outdoor

Kyoto: perfectly straight, slim fruit 40 cm (15 in) long. Smooth skinned with few seeds.

Petite Petino: most finely flavoured and more digestible than other varieties. Vigorous and withstands cool weather but needs using immediately after picking.

LETTUCE

Little Gem (Sugar Cos) is a good choice for the amateur. **Buttercrunch**, a new cabbage type, is crisp and crunchy; stays in good condition long after most varieties have gone to seed.

MARROW

Bush Varieties

Baby Crookneck: early, bright yellow, with curved dumbell 'handles.' Use young for a buttery flavour.

Custard Pie: round, flat, greeny-white with scalloped edges. Wonderful flavour. Excellent at all ages for using hot or cold with stuffing, as an edible container.

Zucchini Hybrid: very early, deep green, slender fruit, similar to courgettes but a heavier cropper. Cut regularly when 7 cm (3 in) or more long to get the plant to keep up a regular flow . . . like milking.

Trailing variety

Vegetable Spaghetti: medium-sized, about 20 cm (8 in) long. Boil or bake the mature fruit, cut in half and the inside comes away and is eaten like spaghetti.

ONION

Red Globe: a renowned 'keeper' till well into April. Glowing deep red outside and when sliced has alternate red and white rings which add a startling note to any winter salad. For cooking, too. Mild flavour.

Welsh Onion (Ciboule): they form thickened and fleshy leaf bases instead of bulbs and can be pulled as spring onions or at any time of the year.

PEAS

Beagle (Hurst): the first wrinkle-seeded early pea with a maturity earlier than some traditional round-seeded types like Meteor or Pilot, which lack the flavour of wrinkle-seeded varieties.

Green Shaft (Hurst): unbeatable for flavour, heavy cropping and behaviour. 0·75 m (2½ ft).

Recette: huge crop with three pods on almost every stem, packed with small sweet and tender peas. Their greatest asset is that they stay that way for weeks, rather than a day, if you cannot pick them regularly.

Victory Freezer: 0·75 m (2½ ft). Extremely heavy cropper, blunt-nosed pods packed with large deep green peas. An all-purpose, delicious variety.

RADISH

Cherry Belle is the sweetest; **Long White Icicle** is early and crisp and does not have a tendency to burst or go hollow inside.

SPINACH

Longstanding Round (summer): the best variety for spring and summer sowing with fleshy dark green leaves.

New Zealand: mildly flavoured and quite unlike ordinary spinach. It forms a low growing creeping plant, with thick arrow-shaped leaves. It will endure hot and dry soils where other varieties fail.

SWEET CORN

Kelvedon Glory: none to beat it for flavour and cropping.

North Star Hybrid: for northern districts. They produce tender, sweet kernels 17–20 cm (7–8 in) long during the most dismal seasons.

TOMATO

Outdoors

Peach (Dobies). Bright yellow medium-sized fruit with a most distinctive flavour and low acid content.

Sugarplum (Gardener's Delight): heavy crop of small to medium sized fruit, absolutely bursting with flavour.

Basic Equipment

Choosing the right tools is the most important step towards actually enjoying using them. The size of your garden, the type of soil and your own size and strength will determine your choice.

Stainless steel tools are the best and most expensive, and invaluable when working on heavy, sticky ground, as they penetrate the soil readily and are easy to clean. Cheap tools are usually of poor quality and unreliable except for the lightest jobs on the lightest soils. A few regularly used, clean, shiny tools are cheaper in the long run than a shedful of misshapen casualties. It is only cheap tools that get left out all night, or accidentally thrown on the bonfire with the rubbish.

Never buy in a hurry. Handle them first to make sure they are the right weight, height or length for you. Choose those which can be used for the greatest variety of purposes, so that you don't have to trundle a barrowful around with you. Remember that the largest tools do not necessarily do the job faster or better, and are more exhausting to use. Above all, buy the best you can afford, choosing the essential ones first. These should be a spade, fork, rake, hoe and hand trowel, gradually adding to them as the budget allows.

SPADE

The most essential tool when starting a new garden. Used mainly for digging, trenching and turning over the soil. Choose one for strength and lightness. There are over 20 different sizes but the home gardener need consider only two: the full-size digging spade and the smaller border version. This is a delight to use and though intended for women is constantly commandeered by the man of the house. The digging spade has a blade of 30 x 19 cm ($11\frac{1}{2}$ x $7\frac{1}{2}$ in), and the smaller one 22 x 14 cm (9 x $5\frac{1}{2}$ in). Use narrow blades for heavy soils.

The handle should have a comfortable grip and shape . . . there are T, D and Y shapes (opposite, centre, right, left), made of various materials apart from wood. Those of durable, weatherproof plastic are probably the best; warm to the touch in cold weather, and easy to clean if you get mud on your hands. Handle shape is a matter of personal preference.

You can get spades with or without a flange on top to protect your footwear. It adds slightly to the weight, and in any case you should always dig in strong shoes or boots.

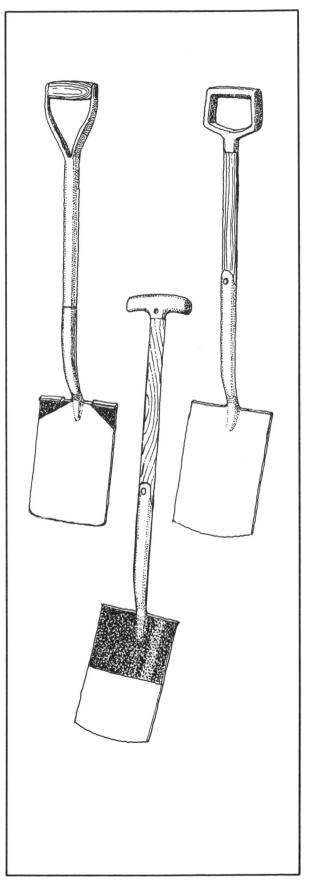

FORK

The garden fork is not a true digging implement. It should be used to break up soil which has already been dug with a spade, by hitting the clods with the back of the fork and then giving them a brisk to-and-fro sweeping with the tips of the teeth. It is also used for loosening a hard surface, working in compost and manure, weeding and lifting crops. Handles are made in varying shapes and materials to suit your grip and taste (opposite, top).

The shape of the teeth (tines or prongs) of a fork affects the ease of work. Most garden shops stock the square-pronged type, but there are also forks with streamlined oval prongs which slip through the soil more easily. As with the spades there are smaller 'border' versions, which are invaluable among the vegetables (opposite, below).

Good garden tools are expensive and repay care. Never put them away dirty. When the soil is sticky and heavy, keep a piece of wood handy to clear the soil from between the prongs of your tools when necessary. Scrape off any remaining mud and wash the steel. When they are dry they should be wiped over with an oily rag and stored in a dry shed until needed again. There are various types of racks with slots or pegs to hold the handles that can be obtained from garden centres and other suppliers; alternatively you can improvise your own. The important thing is to store them off the ground, in dry conditions.

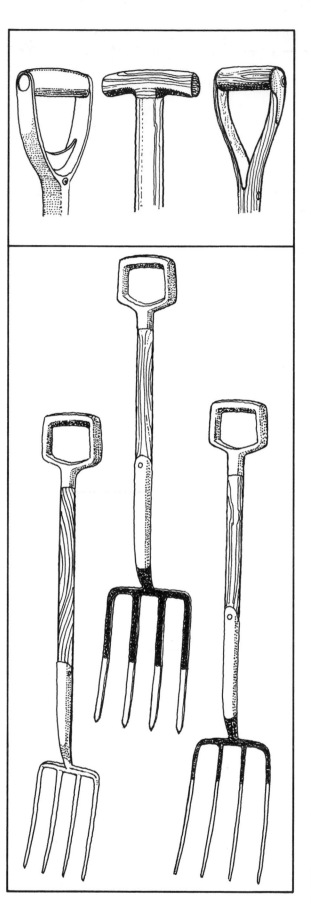

RAKE

Essential for breaking down the soil into a fine tilth before sowing or planting. Also a jack-of-all-trades; areas can be levelled out with it, seed drills can be made by using a side edge with prongs uppermost, and the rake can also be used for working fertilisers thoroughly into the surface. Use it too for lawns and collecting leaves. Go for lightness and a long handle. The number of teeth range from 10 to 16, the more there are the finer the soil surface will become and the more easily and evenly it can be prepared. For general purposes a 12-toothed rake is best (**1**, left). When using, make long sweeping movements, back and forth, and side to side, with the handle about waist high. Avoid always drawing the rake in one direction or you will find it impossible to level the ground.

HOE

Hoes come in a wide variety of shapes and sizes (**2**) and are the most generally used tools in the summer months, to aerate the soil, keep down weeds and to thin out seedlings. There are two main types of hoe. The dutch hoe (**a**) must be used with the blade pushed forward with sliding jabs just beneath the soil surface as you move backwards. The draw hoe (**b** and **c**) has a blade of varying shape set at right angles to the handle and is used with a chopping action as you move forward, treading over soil already worked. The draw hoe is also invaluable for earthing up plants and for opening seed drills, especially wide ones for peas and beans. Various types of modern light hoe (**d** and **e**) are also available.

HAND TROWEL AND FORK

Both excellent for planting, weeding, thinning, lifting seedlings, transplanting. If you can afford only one, choose a trowel (**3**) rather than a fork (**4**). Choose carefully and do make sure the handle is comfortable, to avoid blisters. Blades are in many shapes and handles, usually 12 cm (5 in) or 20 cm (12 in) long. Stainless steel implements are the strongest and easiest to use.

A plastic shoe 'tidy' with separate compartments is handy to keep in the garden shed; it's useful for storing small tools, gardening scissors, etc.

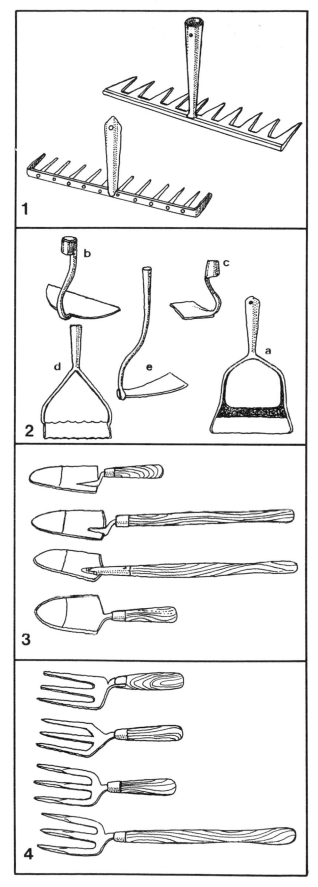

OTHER USEFUL HAND TOOLS

DIBBER
Used for planting leeks, cabbages and other vegetables with long unbranched roots. Bought ones usually have a steel tip to give them a long life (**1**). But you can make one easily from a stout piece of handle.

GARDEN LINE
Essential for straight rows. Easily made with a ball of twine or tarred string, fixed at both ends to sticks and wound up on one of them. A bought swivel type saves time and lasts for ever if you want to go to the expense (**2**).

CULTIVATOR
A hand cultivator (**3, 4, 5**) is valuable for braking up heavy soil for the initial preparation of a seed bed. Also to keep an open soil among rows of vegetables. It is often preferred to a Dutch hoe because it breaks up the soil more deeply. Three-pronged cultivators are the most widely used, though the five-pronged ones are more suitable for a largish area which cannot justify mechanical aids. Use them with a chopping motion; some say work forward, others backward. Do what feels the easier. Available with long handles for rough work, or short ones for close work between plants.

SPECIAL SPADES
These include the 'Claymaster' and 'Ground-breaker' type which are specially designed with four pointed teeth to cope with stiff heavy clay and other rough ground. Particularly useful when reclaiming or starting from scratch (**6**).

Small hand tools have a tiresome habit of vanishing into the weeding trug, and turning up months later minus wooden handle in the bonfire remains. If you coat the handles in violent shades of enamel paint, they will scream out rather than get lost.

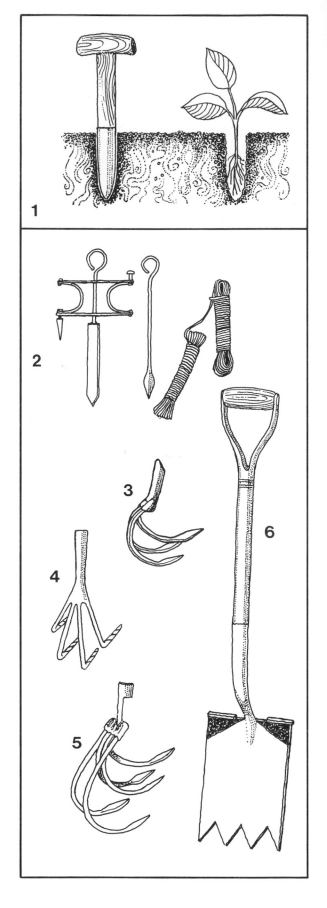

MEASURING STICK

A 1–2 m (3–6 ft) rod or stick, marked at every 7 cm (3 in), is useful for spacing between rows and plants, and can be easily improvised (**1**). Or use your hand tools as measures. If you cannot remember their lengths, mark the handles in some way.

WATERING CAN

This will be in constant use in summer. Test the design carefully, and don't get one which is too heavy when full. The most useful have several nozzle attachments from coarse to fine. Make sure they fit easily but firmly and are not likely to pop off and flood a row of seedlings. Galvanised cans are heavier but last longer than plastic (**2**).

WHEELBARROW

A permanent piece of equipment which you cannot do without if your garden is on the large side. Only you can judge what is right for your needs. The wooden barrow has almost entirely been replaced by those of lighter materials . . . metal alloys, fibreglass, polythene, with solid rubber or cushion tyres (**3**). If you have any distance to 'drive' a barrow, choose the blow-up tyre. Test before you choose. Some of them kick the shins, others overbalance forward. Any respectable garden shop will put a display sack of compost in the barrow for you to test the balance.

Two-wheel handcarts (**4**) may suit some gardens better, but their very lightness can cause a disastrous mess.

Try to avoid watering plants straight from the cold tap. Keep a can — or better still, several cans — filled, in a sunny place, so that the water becomes outdoor 'room' temperature. Whenever practicable, rainwater from a tub should be used in preference to tap water.

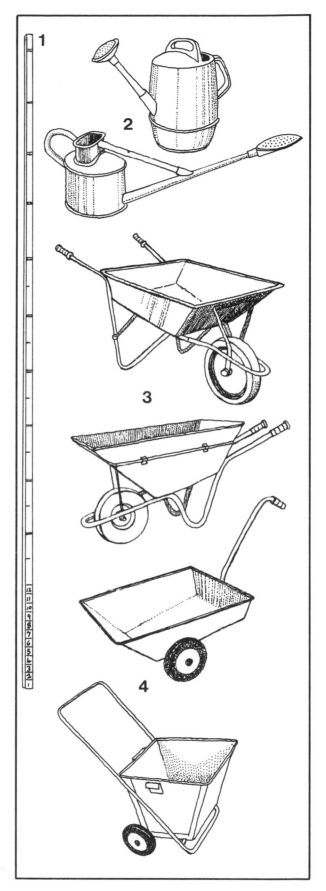

MACHINERY

POWERED CULTIVATOR

A small powered cultivator (**1**) is a great saver of time and effort where the size of the garden justifies the expense (around $\frac{1}{3}$ acre or more). Consider how much work there is to be done in the garden as a whole. If there is much digging, mowing of rough grass and hedge trimming, it would be worth buying the various attachments available. They can break down the soil in spring, chop in manure, weed between rows. Peas and dwarf beans can be cleared quickly after picking, the beds rapidly tilled and fresh seeds put in.

Warning The garden must be planned and tailored for the machine, rather than the other way round. Choose the cultivator which most suits your needs . . . most have working widths from about 22 cm (9 in). Then arrange your rows, *straight,* so that both cultivator wheels and heads can get between them without damaging tops or roots of the plants. *Leave room* for turning the machine at each end of the rows – about twice the length of the machine.

HANDY AIDS

CLOCHES

The advantages of using cloches are that crops can be sown, planted and harvested earlier and also later, as they are protected from cold winds and frost, and that you can grow half-hardy 'luxury' vegetables without the expense of a greenhouse. The disadvantages are that they are rather fiddly and time-consuming; they make it more difficult to deal with weeds, and to harvest the crops. The cloches themselves must be looked after; they should be carefully cleaned and stacked when not in use.

Plastic Cheaper and more easily handled than glass. Light, easy to store and almost unbreakable. Many kinds and shapes (**2**, **3**, **4**) – some rigid, others made of continuous length of plastic 'tunnel' and supported at intervals by wire hoops. Others again are made of wire-enforced plastic. The main disadvantage is keeping them tethered in the wind.

Tender plants such as sweetcorn can be protected from cold winds by encircling each plant with a couple of cloches stood on end and tied round with twine.

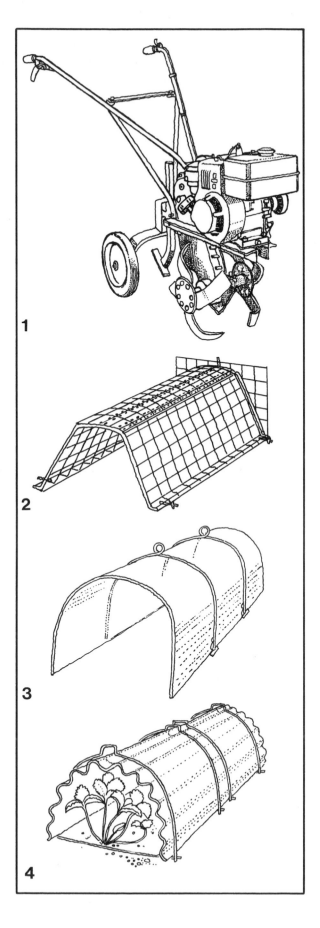

1

2

3

4

Glass The most popular types are of two basic shapes known as the tent and the barn (**1, 2**). The tent types are used for raising seedlings or protecting a single row of crops at an early stage, for they lack headroom. The barn types are more versatile, usually 61 cm (2 ft) long and 58 cm (23 in) wide. Heights vary from roughly 30 cm–48 cm (12–19 in). Both can be bought single or in sets of 12. Glass cloches are more difficult to assemble than plastic types. You need a skilled DIY man on hand till you get the knack.

FRAMES

Many different types, homemade and bought, each with its individual qualities. The main difference is whether the frame has solid sides (**3**) or is entirely of glass or plastic (**4**). For maximum protection in cold exposed places, a frame with wooden or brick sides is best. The more glass used, the more heat is lost. The frame should face south when possible, in a sheltered, yet open, place away from shadows and overhanging trees.

Good and Bad Points Steel designs are strong and heavily galvanised to prevent rusting, but the tops ('lights') are rather heavy and difficult for a woman to open and shut. Aluminium frames are light and smaller ones portable so they can be moved around and stored in winter. Very easy and adaptable. Brick frames are not popular for the average-sized garden because of their most worthy feature . . . permanence. They are relatively expensive to build and you can't take them with you if you have to move.

The home handyman can make his own from wood, asbestos, junkyard window frames or skylights. *Beware* if using plastic instead of glass for top 'lights'. It must be rigid or rain will form individual lakes and sink it.

An economical way to use a frame is to grow a number of different vegetables at the same time, each in its own seedbox filled with special seed compost. As each vegetable gets ready for planting out, its box can be lifted out and replaced by a box of a later-growing vegetable.

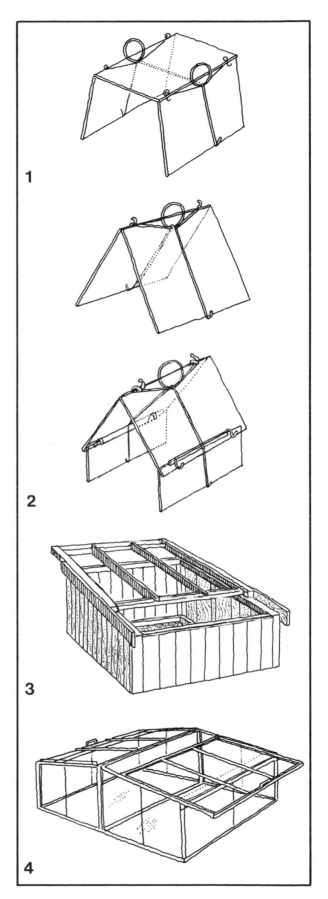

1

2

3

4

POTS AND TRAYS

The old clay pots and wooden seed boxes have now been almost entirely superseded by plastic ones (**1**). They are light, strong, easy to clean and store, more hygienic and less breakable.

Caution   Don't overwater plastic pots. They dry out less quickly than clay.

Fibre pots   These are made from sterilised peat and wood pulp with plant food added. Particularly good for seeds raised in a frame or in the house which resent root disturbance when they later go into open ground. Sweet corn and marrows are good examples. When frosts are over you plant the lot, seedlings and pots. The roots feed on and eventually grow right through the peat-based fibre. All shapes and sizes to suit your needs (**2**).

Caution   Keep them well watered, particularly when planting them out into dry soil.

NETTING

Some kind of netting is necessary to protect your vegetables from birds. A single dawn raid can rob you of a crop you have nurtured for months, such as sprouts, or an expensive row of pea or bean seed. They can attack at all stages . . . newly sown seed, seedlings, leaves, pods and maturing crops almost ready to harvest. Pigeons are perhaps the worst offenders, but it depends on where you live and also on local bird tastes.

   Prevention is essential as there is no cure once the damage is done. Wire, nylon, or plastic coated wire are more durable than cotton or fishnet (**3, 4**).

> If you are still using old clay pots, remember that they need to be well scrubbed before re-using, to avoid transferring contamination from previously infected soil. They must also be thoroughly soaked before refilling with new soil.

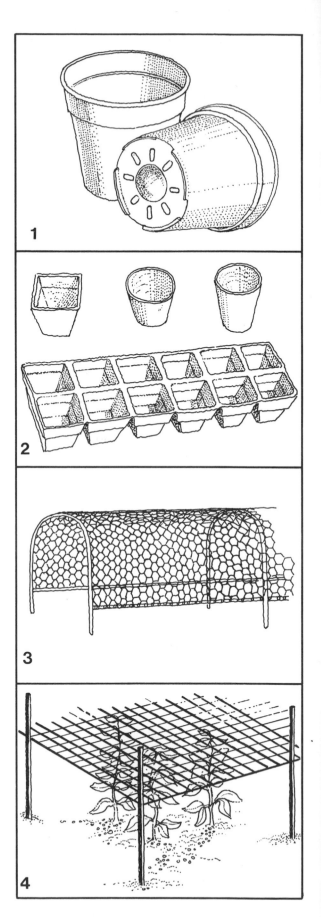

Plastic netting comes in all sizes and weights of mesh, is easy to handle and store, and almost indestructible (**1**).

SUPPORTS

These range from pea sticks (cut from scrub land or hedgerows), bamboo canes, makeshift runner bean 'ladders' of twine between supporting poles, to long lasting rigid or flexible polythene (**2, 3**). Get the best you can afford and the least offensive to the eye.

Whatever you use, make sure it is firmly tethered, particularly at the ends of the rows. Vegetables can be as decorative as flowers, but not when they are blown over carrying a heavy crop.

Pea sticks are often covered with fungus spores by the end of the season and must be burnt. All wooden stakes have this disadvantage. Bamboo canes are more hygenic, light, strong and easy to store (**4**). Some crops not generally considered staking candidates often need help in exposed gardens. Examples are the larger greens, broad beans, sweet corn. They can be supported so their roots are not rocked and damaged by putting a stake at each end of the row, and running twine or plastic covered wire alone, between the plants from one to the other.

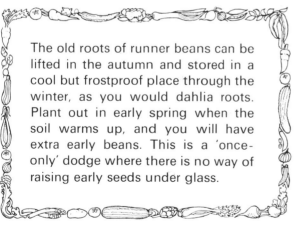

The old roots of runner beans can be lifted in the autumn and stored in a cool but frostproof place through the winter, as you would dahlia roots. Plant out in early spring when the soil warms up, and you will have extra early beans. This is a 'once-only' dodge where there is no way of raising early seeds under glass.

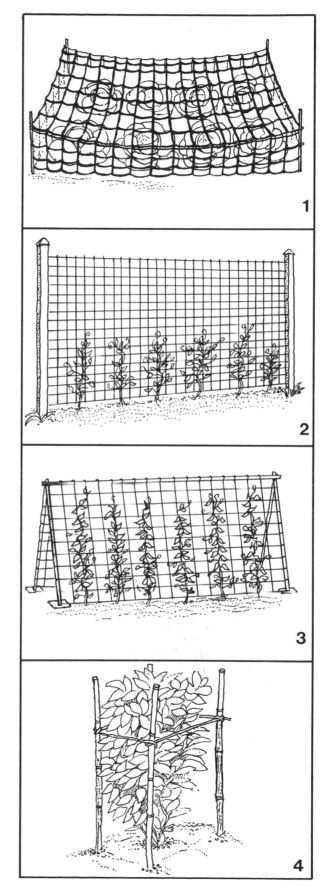

Natural and Artificial Aids

COMPOST

You **must** have a compost heap if you grow things, to convert garden waste into a feast for the next crops, and a soil structure to keep them in fitness and health. Some people say that no seedling weeds or diseased plants should go onto it, but the heat of a properly made compost heap will be enough to kill all the weed seeds, pests and diseases too.

The rule to remember is that 'everything that has lived can live again in another plant'. Because of the shortage of manure, compost has become a necessity but there is no need to be obsessed with it or to worry about turning it constantly.

CHOOSING A SITE

Choose a convenient corner of earth, preferably sheltered from high winds, driving rain or scorching sun; beneath a small, leafy tree is a good spot. To keep it tidy and compact, construct some kind of enclosure measuring at least 1.20 m (4 ft) square. Wire netting fixed on stakes will prevent the compost from sprawling and let in the essential air. In small gardens it is simplest to make the heaps in strong galvanised wire or plastic netting (see opposite), or open wooden bins (below, right).

What to put on your compost heap? It can digest almost anything in the right proportions and properly prepared.

Waste from your garden	Waste from your house
Grass cuttings	Vegetable peelings
Soft hedge clippings and prunings	Mouldy fruit
Chopped up vegetable stalks	Tea leaves and coffee grains
Dead flowers, bolted or finished crops	Carpet sweepings
Weeds, leaves, straw	Waste greenstuff
Animal manure (including pets')	Vacuum cleaner contents
Stored crops gone rotten	Crushed egg shells
General garden debris	Sodden paper
	Natural fibre rags
	Human hair, pet combings

Unsuitable for Compost Diet

Anything contaminated with oil or creosote

Hardwood or shavings

Man-made fibres

Grass cuttings from the first mowing after using
weedkiller

Fat, bones and cooked left-overs (could attract
rats)

Tough or evergreen leaves

HOW TO MAKE YOUR COMPOST HEAP

The base of the heap can be coarser than the rest,
to give air and good drainage: artichoke stems, the
finished haulms of runner beans, interspersed
with old woollies, ragged tea cloths and elderly
dressing gowns.

Never put on a solid layer of anything, whether
lawn mowings or bolted lettuce plants. Keep the
ingredients mixed and varied. If the mixture is dry,
wet it. If coarse and open, trample on it to make it
compact, but not so heavily that air cannot get
through.

Each layer of compost, which should be
between 15–23 cm (6–9 in), needs an application
of an activator to accelerate the natural rotting
process. This can be a 2–3 cm (1 in) layer of
manure, a sprinkling of dried blood or a proprietary
product such as ADCO, GAROTTA etc, used strictly
to the makers' instructions. This is best followed
by a sprinkling of topsoil to check evaporation and
help decomposition (see cross section).

Don't bother to shake the soil from the roots of
pulled up weeds or crops before putting them on
the heap; it all helps in the rotting process.

Your compost should be ready in 8–12 weeks,
though it takes a little longer during winter
months. To tell when the compost is 'cooked', dig
your fork into the heap which should be black,
crumbly, and sweet smelling. Use any unrotted
stuff to start a new heap. You will soon discover
which types of rubbish can't be used, such as
nylon tights and bottle tops. Light soils prefer well
rotted compost to turn them into good loams,
while heavier soils need it less rotted to help
lighten them with coarser material.

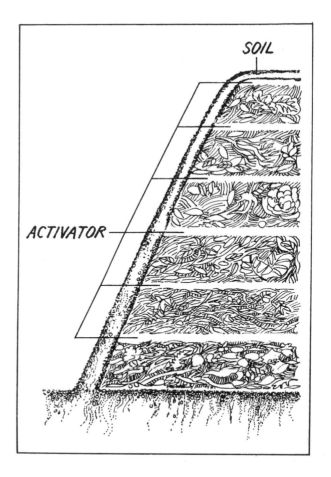

SOIL

ACTIVATOR

FERTILISERS

It is not possible to grow good vegetables without using some organic manures, which have a plant or animal origin and release their plant food slowly. This is important for those vegetables which take a year or more to mature. Organic fertilisers include bone meal, hoof and horn meal, fish meal, dried blood, farmyard manure, compost, seaweed and used hops. Inorganic fertilisers are manufactured and quick-acting. They include sulphate of ammonia, superphosphate of lime and sulphate of potash, which the plants readily lap up. But they must be used strictly according to the makers' instructions, or they can cause damage and death. Any lumps must be broken up or the application will be uneven (1). Skilled gardeners use individual chemicals for particular crops, but it is safer for the amateur to buy compound proprietary fertilisers for general use from any garden shop.

Fertilisers can be applied dry (2) or in solution. Dry fertilisers should always be kept off leaves as much as possible. Since plants can only take minerals from the soil in solution, liquid fertilisers act more rapidly than dry ones, unless they are watered in, or there is rain. A liquid feed can be made by placing animal manure in a sacking bag and suspending this in a large container filled with water; after a few days the resulting thick liquid can be diluted for use (3). Some dilute liquid fertilisers can be applied to the leaves as well as the soil (4), a process known as 'foliar feeding'; this can bring an almost immediate improvement.

Ash from the bonfire will give potash to growing plants, but it soon loses its value and should be used fresh. Soot is just the opposite and must be stacked in the open for at least three months before it can be used as a general fertiliser.

The chart on page 49 is a guide to different types of fertilisers, and the correct method of application. A base dressing is dug into the soil before planting and goes to the roots; a top dressing is scattered on the ground after the plant has started to grow.

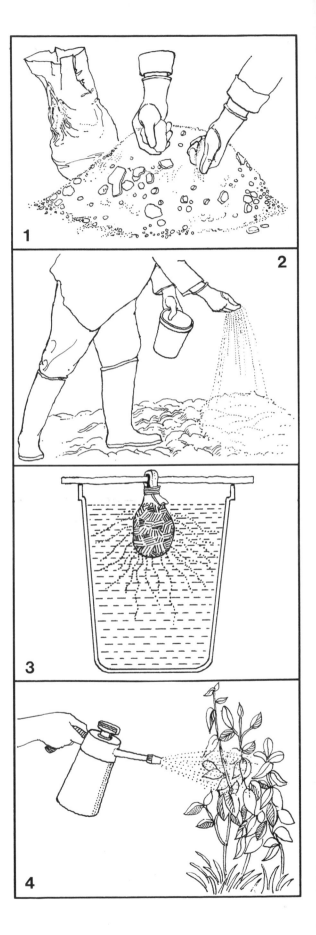

ORGANIC

Fertiliser	Action	Application
Bone meal	Slow	Pre-planting base dressing; surface scatter, work in
Dried blood	Medium; lasting	Top dressing during growth; surface scatter, work in
Farmyard manure	Slow	Base dressing, summer and spring mulch; work in later
Fish meal	Rapid	As top dressing, surface scatter, work in
Hoof and horn	Slow	Pre-planting base dressing; surface scatter, work in
Poultry manure	Continuous during growth	Spring, 2–3 weeks before sowing, or as top dressing; surface scatter, work in
Seaweed	Slow	Pre-planting base dressing; surface scatter, work in
Sewage sludge	Slow	As above
Soot	Fairly rapid	Pre-planting base dressing; top dressing during growth; scatter and rake in after weathering
Used hops	Slow	Pre-planting base dressing; surface scatter, work in
Wood ash	Fairly rapid	Spring, before planting; surface scatter, work in.

INORGANIC

Fertiliser	Action	Application
Nitro-chalk	Fairly rapid	Top dressing during growth; surface scatter, work in
Sulphate of ammonia	Rapid	Spring, pre-planting; top dressing during growth; surface scatter, work in
Sulphate of potash	Steady and continuous	Spring, pre-planting; surface scatter, work in
Super-phosphate of lime	Medium	Spring, pre-planting, or top dressing; surface scatter, work in.

WEED CONTROL

In spite of their time-saving advantages, be wary when using chemical weedkillers among anything you are going to eat. The safest implements for keeping down weeds are a fork (**1**), hoe (**2**) or mulch – a layer of organic material which helps to smother the weeds, among other useful functions (**3**). Properly prepared ground should already have had deep-rooted perennial weeds removed, but the odd ones which appear must be dug out.

Old-fashioned hoeing, in spite of all chemical advances, is still the best way to kill seedling weeds, as well as being good for most crops by letting in air.

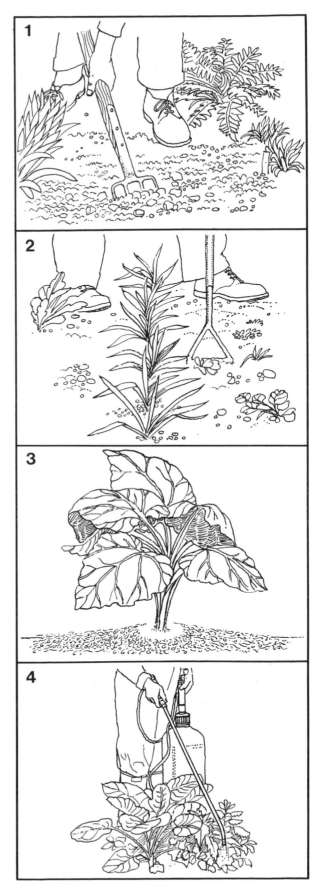

GOLDEN RULES FOR DEALING WITH WEEDS

1 Hoe them when they are still very young and the soil dry.
2 Pull them up before they take over the ground.
3 Cut them before they go to seed.
4 Never let big weeds grow with small plants.
5 Burn those which are deep-rooting, gone to seed or spread quickly, and make use of healthy ones by composting.

MULCHING

All kinds of mulches can be used between vegetable rows and around individual plants. They help to prevent annual weed seeds from germinating; keep the soil cool and moist, and cut out the need for hoeing and watering except in droughts. Mulches should be at least 3 cm (an inch or so) deep; they can be formed of grass cuttings, old manure, peat, damp newspapers, compost, sawdust, wool 'shoddy', straw etc. Keep them away from the stems of the plants. Strips of black polythene between rows serve the same purpose but have the disadvantage of looking unsightly; they have to be securely anchored at the edges, tend to collect puddles and cannot be used as a 'path' when you want to harvest the crop.

CHEMICAL TREATMENTS

WEEDOL is the only total weedkiller suitable for use among vegetables, because it works through the leaves of the plant weeds and has no effect at all on the soil. It is best applied with a special applicator fitted with a narrow sprinkling bar which can be held close to the ground away from the vegetable leaves, but over the leaves of young weeds (4, page 49). As with all garden chemicals, stick to the printed instructions and don't alter the recommended dosage. *Wash out containers several times, after use; store the preparation, clearly labelled, out of the way of children and old people.*

Weed Preventers There are several proprietary makes, sold in measured sachets to be dissolved in water. They catch weeds as the seed germinates and remain active in the ground for up to 10 weeks; they should therefore be used only once per crop. The disadvantage of this method is that weed preventers usually have to be applied to ground already free of weeds; they control all annual weeds which start from seed, but are powerless against perennials which grow from remains of roots. *Food crops should never be gathered within 8 weeks of the last treatment.*

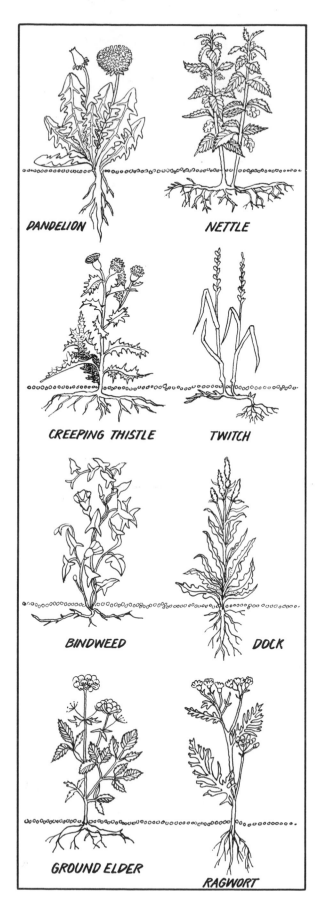

DANDELION

NETTLE

CREEPING THISTLE

TWITCH

BINDWEED

DOCK

GROUND ELDER

RAGWORT

Pests, Diseases and Cures

Well grown plants are less likely to be laid low, or made inedible by pests and diseases, than starved, poorly grown ones. But good cultivation cannot guarantee immunity. Pests and diseases arrive and take off with the season, their incidence varying in intensity from year to year, according to weather conditions.

Most plant foes can easily be banished by spraying if the trouble is not allowed to reach serious proportions. The sooner you act the less damage there will be. Keep a sharp look out.

Manufacturers have prepared a number of multi-purpose sprays and dusts which make mixing and preparing foolproof *only* if instructions are read carefully and carried out exactly.

It is particularly important when dealing with food crops to leave the correct periods of time between application and harvesting. This information is given in the table on page 59 which lists the pesticides, fungicides, etc recommended in this chapter and includes other precautionary notes.

The range of sprayers now should suit all purposes and pockets, but take care to wash them out well and do not allow them to be used for other purposes.

Once again, *keep all chemicals stored out of reach of children, old people whose sight may be failing, and pets; never decant chemicals into bottles which could lead to them being mistaken for soft drinks.*

PESTS

APHIDS

Sometimes known as greenfly, blackfly, blue bug etc. A large family of plant lice which will attack all members of the cabbage family, as well as peas, beans etc. They generally attack young shoots and the undersides of young leaves and weaken plants by sucking the sap. Leaves become distorted and fall prematurely, which checks the growth (see opposite).

Cure Spray with Malathion, Menazon, or Derris when an attack is noticed. Make sure the chemical lands directly on the aphids.

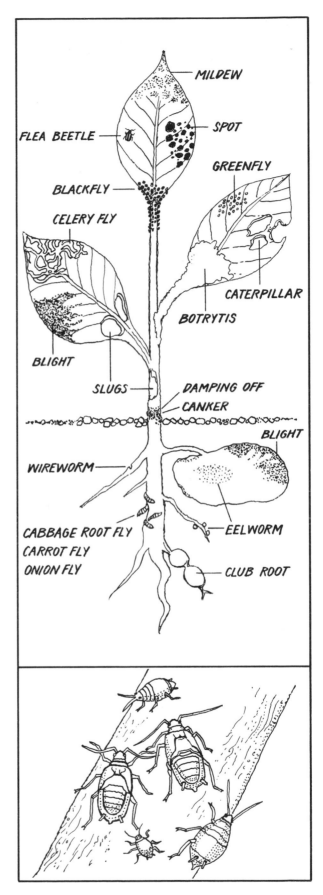

Blackfly are particularly partial to young broad bean growth (**1**). They can usually be controlled by sowing early and pinching out the growing tips when the flowers have been set.

CABBAGE CATERPILLARS
These are the larvae of the white butterfly which flits about the cabbage bed laying enormous numbers of eggs, on the undersurfaces of cabbage and other brassica leaves. The caterpillars which hatch out are green, have voracious appetites and can turn the plants into skeletons in a few days if not checked (**2**).

Cure Spray or dust the plants with Derris or Carbaryl. The most effective method where possible is to pick them off by hand.

CABBAGE ROOT FLY
The small white maggots are found on the stems of brassica plants just below ground level in early summer. They burrow down to attack the plant. Newly planted seedlings are particularly vulnerable to attack (**3**).

Cure Cut discs 8 cm (3 in) square out of tarred felt. Cut a slit in the middle of one side to the centre of the disc. Slip the disc round the base of the stem so that it lies flat on the soil. The flies will be unable to reach the roots to lay their eggs, which usually occurs from May onwards. Alternatively dust the seedbed with Gamma BHC and newly planted seedlings with 4 per cent calomel dust, repeating the application two weeks later.

CARROT FLY
A small shiny bottle-green fly which lays eggs in the soil along carrot rows during spring and summer. The small white maggots hatch out and burrow into the roots, often to the extent of making them worthless (**4**). This pest is most troublesome in late April and through May. Carrots sown in June and July often escape unscathed because few flies are about then.

Cure Dust Naphthalene on the surface soil around plants every ten days, from thinning time till the end of June; or in the early seedling stages dust with Gamma BHC.

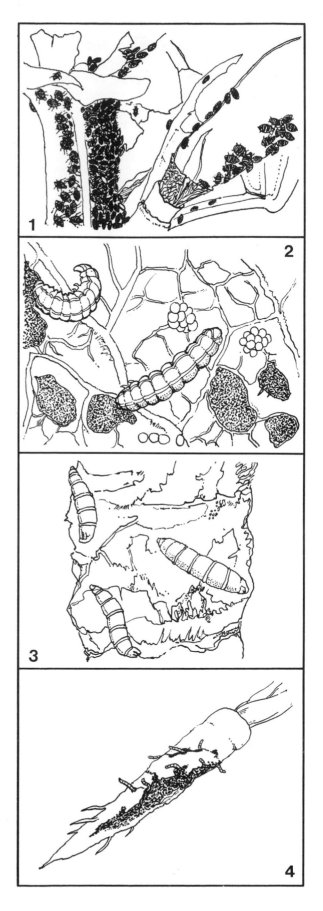

CELERY FLY

The small fly lays her eggs on the undersides of the celery leaves during spring and summer, and immediately they hatch the tiny white or green grubs work their way into the leaf tissues to feed. This creates whitish blisters or trails (**1**) which have given the alternative name for this pest of 'celery leaf miner'. A bad attack of tunnelling takes all the veins from the leaves with only skin remaining.

Cure Mild attacks can be controlled by picking off and burning affected leaves. Or spray occasionally from May to August with Malathion or BHC (**2**).

EELWORMS

Roots, bulbs and tubers can be attacked by these microscopic creatures both underground and in their leaves. They produce tiny white cysts on potato roots (**3**) which turn the leaves yellow and check growth; the cysts can also re-infect clean soil. When onions are attacked the eelworms pass to the stems from the bulbs and cause swelling and misshapen growth (**4**).

Cure Where soil becomes contaminated, the crop concerned should not be grown in that piece of ground for several years. Destroy all infected plants and keep down weeds, particularly chickweed, which acts as host for the onion eelworm.

One way to cut down pests and diseases is to take care not to leave rubbish about in the garden, to become a breeding ground for slugs, woodlice etc. Burn old boxes and badly diseased material and compost the rest.

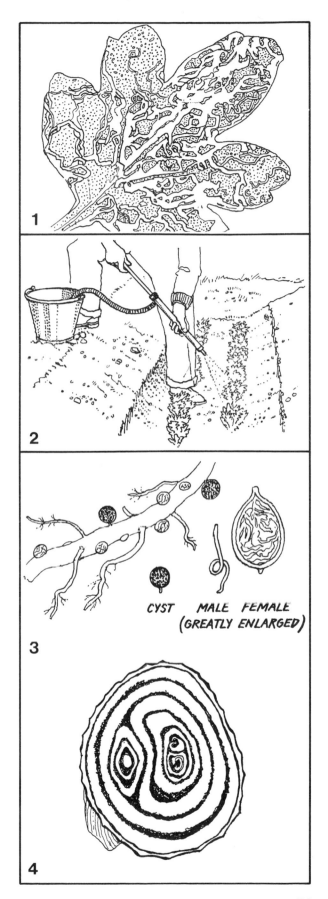

1

2

CYST   MALE FEMALE
(GREATLY ENLARGED)

3

4

FLEA BEETLE

Small blackish beetle about 3 mm ($\frac{1}{8}$ in) long (**1**), which jumps a long way when disturbed. They attack seedlings and young cabbage and brassicas, turnip and radish, eating small round holes in the leaves and entirely ruining them if not checked. Most trouble is caused on light sandy soils in dry weather. Not nearly such a problem in dull or damp weather.

Cure Dust the seedlings occasionally with Gamma BHC, Derris or Malathion. It helps to prevent attack if seedlings can grow quickly and vigorously; encourage them by watering, hoeing and using artificial fertilisers.

MICE

They often do extensive damage to early sown peas and beans. Whole rows of newly sown or just germinated seed can be wrecked overnight (**2**).

Cure Provided there are no young children around use a proprietary mouse poison between the rows. It must be kept dry and concealed from pets and birds; tuck it away under raised tiles, or in a small piece of piping.

ONION FLY

One of the worst pests in the garden, rather like a small house fly. It lays eggs in spring and summer near the bottom of young onion plants. The white maggots burrow to the bottom of the bulb and feed, making it unusable. First indication of attack is that the foliage turns yellow and flags.

Cure Dust the soil with BHC or Lindane immediately after planting and again two weeks later to discourage an attack (**3**). Remove and burn damaged plants. When hoeing among onions be most careful not to damage the plants, as the flies will be attracted to the smell.

A trick which often works is to grow carrots and onions in alternate rows. The smell of the one keeps away the pest of the other.

PIGEONS

Mainly a menace to brassica crops (the cabbage family) in the autumn and winter. They are not scared for long by strips of tinfoil or red-painted bottles.

Cure The only certain one is to switch your fruit netting over to them, or to buy nylon netting in the widths and lengths which suit your planting plan the best (**4**).

54

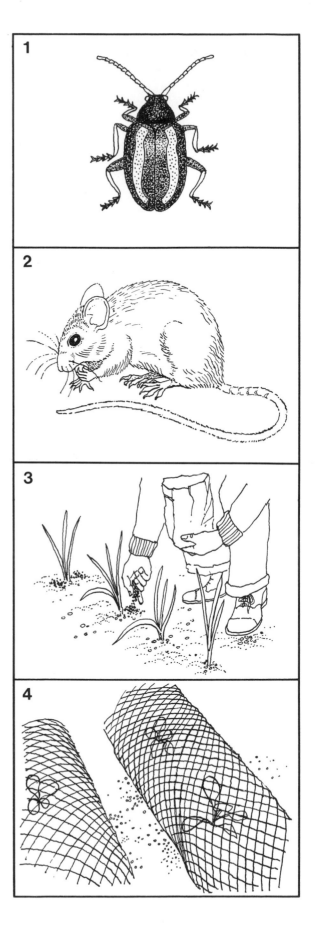

SLUGS

They do great damage to celery, especially, and the cabbage family. They feed above ground during the night, attacking seedlings and young plants, and below the ground any time they fancy (**1** and **2**). They dislike frost or dry soil, and burrow down deeply when these conditions occur.

In the case of potatoes, the slug is not a specific pest to this crop if it is grown in well cultivated soil. But slugs can ruin much of the crop if weedy wasteland is taken over for cultivation and potatoes planted as one of the first crops. (So much for the myth that 'potatoes clear the ground'.) Slugs seldom damage first early potatoes being dug in June and July. But later varieties show slug damage by having holes tunnelled into the tubers. These can be used for cooking (with the offending parts cut out) but should never be stored.

Cure   There are various methods: use slug bait, carefully keeping to the maker's instructions or use a soil fumigant such as Naphthalene. Alternatively (a safer choice if there are young children or pets around) use a mulch; when sedge peat or compost is used as a mulch round the plants the slugs cannot move about and die. They need to get under the sheets of a cool soil to stay healthy. (For instructions on mulching, see page 50.)

WIREWORMS

This insect is the grub of the click beetle (**3**) and may live in the soil for about six years before turning into a beetle. They injure crops below ground by destroying smaller roots and boring tunnels into larger ones. This damage can be severe in spring and early autumn (**4**).

Cure   Bury pieces of potato or carrot attached to wooden sticks 2–3 cm (1 in) deep close to the crops and examine frequently. Kill any wireworms that have burrowed and set another trap. They can be deterred by forking in Naphthalene or, where there is no danger of tainting carrot or potato crops, killed by dusting soil with BHC.

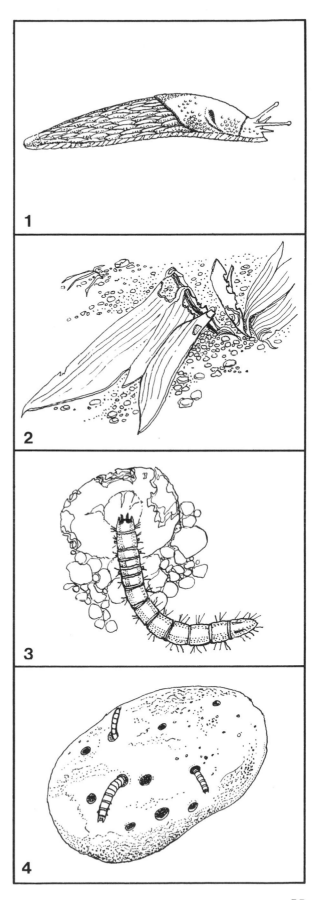

1

2

3

4

DISEASES

BOTRYTIS

'Grey mould', the common name for this disease, comes from the grey spores of the fungus which forms a mould on the leaves and stems of the plants. The attacked parts decay (1).

Cure Crops should be gathered before the weather becomes damp and cold, and stored in dry, airy places. Spray with Thiram or a systemic fungicide.

BROAD BEAN CHOCOLATE SPOT

A form of botrytis which is seen as dark brown blotches on the leaves, and streaks on the stems (2). More severe after very cold or wet weather and is therefore more common on autumn-sown beans than on those sown early in the year. Treat as above.

CELERY LEAF SPOT

The fungus causing this disease is carried on seed, but all reputable seedsmen sell seed which has been treated against it. The disease shows up as brown spots on the leaves which wither and die (3). It spreads rapidly in damp weather.

Cure Spray with a copper fungicide or Zineb as soon as the disease is seen and repeat at fortnightly intervals until October.

CLUB ROOT

One of the best known vegetable diseases, it affects cabbages and other brassicas, making the roots swollen, distorted and almost fibreless. These eventually decay amid an evil smell. Infected plants must be burnt and the soil should not be used for any crops susceptible to the disease for at least four years. Farmyard manure can be a means of bringing the disease into the garden if the animals providing it have been fed on swedes or any member of the brassica family which has been affected by club root. (See illustration of this disease on page 12.)

Cure Acid soil is particularly vulnerable to the disease and should be limed (4) at the rate of 250 g (9 oz) per sq m ($1\frac{1}{4}$ sq yd) as soon as the infected plants have been cleared. Similar dressings should be given annually for 3 or 4 years.

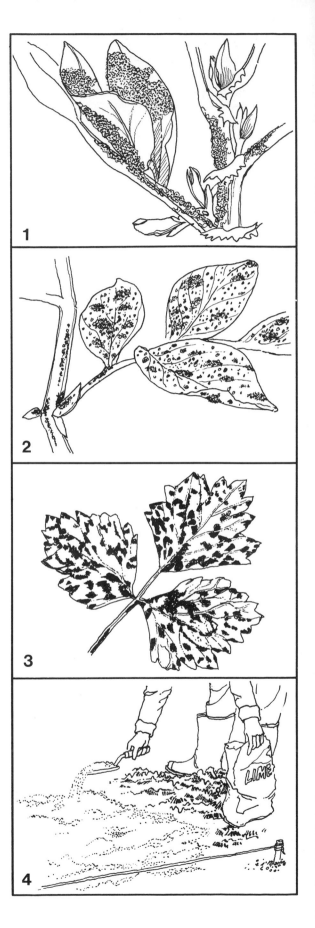

'DAMPING OFF'

This fungal disease attacks seedlings brought up under glass. They collapse in their pots and boxes as the disease attacks just above soil level (**1**). It is most likely to happen where seeds are sown too thickly and it spreads quickly in damp, stuffy conditions.

Cure Sow thinly and prick off as soon as possible. Use sterilised compost; water seedlings with copper fungicide or dust with Captan.

MILDEW

A fungal disease which attacks a variety of crops. It is most likely to occur when the atmosphere is moist and the soil rather dry, and is common in August and September. The surfaces of the leaves, pods and sometimes stems, become covered with white or grey patches that often appear mealy (**2**). Plants are weakened rather than killed.

Cure Spray regularly with Dinocap if disease appears. Keep plants well watered. Brassicas, lettuce, onions, spinach and peas are most likely to be attacked.

PARSNIP CANKER

Brown, or sometimes black patches are seen around the top of the roots, which may crack. Wet rot sets in and soon destroys the root completely (**3**).

Cure Where the trouble has happened before, give the soil plenty of lime before sowing the seed. Do not grow parsnips on heavily manured ground. Canker is sometimes sparked off by injuries originally caused by the carrot fly larvae.

If, despite all your efforts, 'damping off' has occurred among your seedlings, it is best to cut your losses and re-sow in fresh pots or boxes filled with fresh soil.

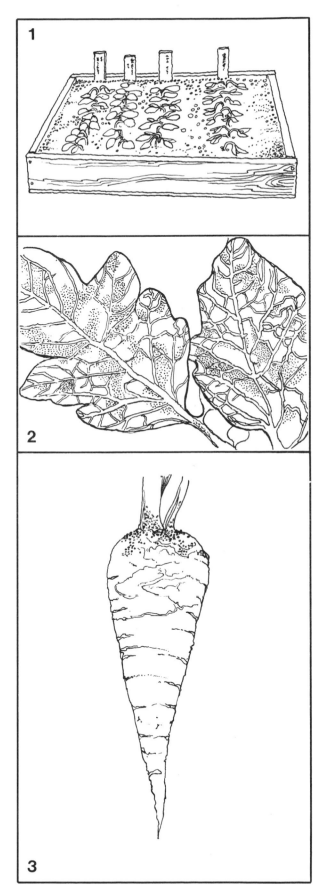

POTATO BLIGHT

This disease attacks both potatoes and tomatoes, causing moist black or brown patches on these leaves (**1** and **2**). These spread rapidly to the stems which eventually die. Potato tubers turn brown and rot (**3**); tomato fruits become marked with decaying patches and also rot (**2**). The disease can spread at an alarming rate. It is unlikely to cause trouble on early varieties, as it does not usually strike plants till the beginning of July. The damage is light in dry seasons, but can be devastating in a mild wet summer.

Cure Apply a preventative spray of a copper fungicide or Zineb (**4**) early in July, and at fortnightly intervals until the middle of September.

What is 'humus'?

All gardening books refer to this mysterious substance, often assuming, over-confidently, that the reader understands what is meant. Humus is the organic matter in soil, the presence of which in sufficient quantities is essential to the building up and sustaining of fertility; without humus soil is merely finely ground rock. Humus is formed by the gradual decomposition of plant and animal remains, brought about by hordes of living and dead bacteria. It assists fertility because as a result of chemical action of these micro-organisms, it supplies vital nitrate to the plants, and because it retains moisture which helps to break up the soil.

How to supply humus? There are many different humus-makers which fall into two basic types; the 'raw' and the 'matured'. Raw humus is formed from grass clippings, straw and weeds dug into the surface, before they are decomposed by bacteria. Mature humus has already been composted and has a longer life in the soil. This type includes well-rotted manure, peat, hop manure and of course garden compost (see page 47). A 'raw' humus maker is transformed into a matured one by composting.

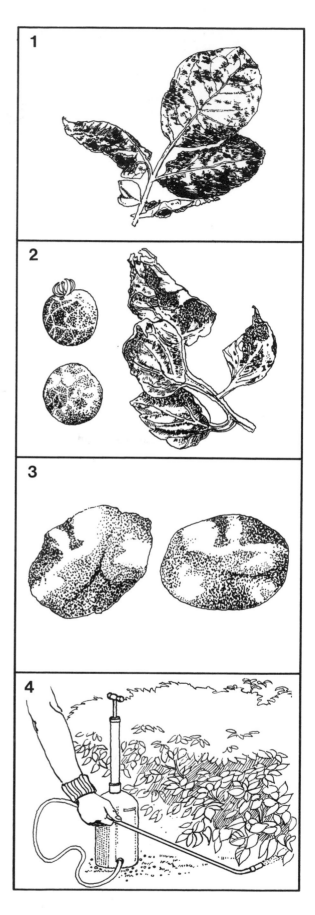

REMEDIES FOR PESTS AND DISEASES

The following preparations are recommended in the preceding pages. For readers who are growing flowers and fruit along with their vegetables, some reminders relating to these are included under 'Special comments'.

Chemical	Spray or Dust	Length of time before harvesting	Special comments
Bordeaux mixture	Liquid and dust	2 weeks	Leaves deposit. Don't use in cold, damp conditions or may harm foliage
Calomel	Wettable dust	1 month	Harmful to fish
Captan	Wettable powder	1 week	Do not use on fruit for preserving or freezing
Carbaryl	Wettable powder	1 week	Harmful to bees and fish
Copper fungicides	Wettable powders	3 weeks	Harmful to fish and livestock
Derris	Available in both forms	1 day	Harmful to fish
Dinocap	Wettable powder	1 week	Harmful to fish
Gamma BHC and Lindane	Liquid and dust	2 weeks	Do not use on cucumbers or marrows
Malathion	Liquid	7 days	Keep away from sweet peas, ferns, petunias, zinnias, antirrhinums
Menazon	Liquid	3 weeks	Harmful to bees and livestock
Naphthalene	Granules	1-2 days	Acts as a deterrent — like mothballs
Systemic fungicide (Benomyl)	Wettable powder	Follow makers' instructions	—
Thiram	Wettable powder	1 week	Do not use on fruit for freezing
Weedol	Granules	not applicable	Weedkiller which is inactivated on contact with soil
Zineb	Wettable powder	1 week	Allow 1 month before harvesting blackcurrants to avoid tainting

Note: Most garden chemicals are safe to use if handled sensibly. *The makers' instructions must be followed strictly.* Keep all chemicals under lock and key and in a place not easily accessible to children and animals. Don't forget that an old person's failing sight can lead to dangerous mistakes occurring, and never decant chemicals into soft drinks bottles.

Harvesting Your Crops

Home-grown vegetables are very often wasted because they are not harvested at the right time. With the present price of seeds it is no consolation to feed them to the compost heap instead of the family. It is true that it takes longer to harvest and prepare small young vegetables, and you need more of them, than if you wait till crops are fully mature; but the difference in flavour is indescribable. Also, if you wait for most of a crop to mature, some vegetables are obviously going to be too tough or long in the tooth to eat at all.

Some produce is often wasted too, because the grower does not realise that a number of vegetables are dual purpose and a few treble, so that almost all the plant can be eaten at different times.

ARTICHOKE

GLOBE
Cut the main head while it is still young (**1**), before the base swells to resemble a cottage loaf. Leave a 15 cm (6 in) stem so it can be stood in water to stay fresh if not wanted immediately. The main heads are always the best. Cut the small side buds (**2**) when they are about the size of a hen's egg and use whole. It is best to cut them an hour before cooking and wash them well; earwigs and insects get down among the scales.

JERUSALEM
The tubers are hardy and can be left in the ground until needed in winter, although frozen or muddy soil makes it difficult to lift them just when you might want them. Lift them in autumn (**3**) and store in covered boxes (**4**); or lift a few to store for when the ground is undiggable, and leave some in the open. The advantage of leaving the whole crop in the ground is that freshly dug tubers have a far better flavour than stored ones. Take care not to damage the tubers when lifting or the 'wound' will go brown. Set aside some of the medium-sized ones for replanting the following year.

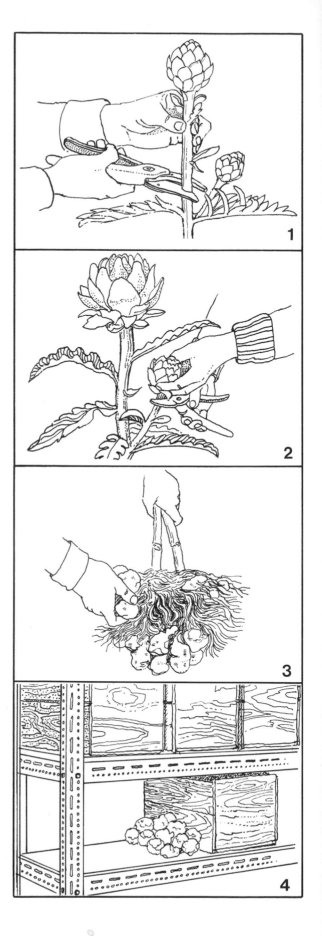

ASPARAGUS

Use a sharp, narrow knife. When the tips are 7–10 cm (3–4 in) above the soil, cut the spears well below the ground, about 2–3 cm (2 in) above the crowns (**1**) Take care, because new shoots will be continually coming up from the hidden crown and you may slice them off. If you prefer the taste of green asparagus, let the spears grow taller and cut them off at ground level. Cut every two days when it first starts to grow (usually early May) and every day when the weather gets warmer. Stop cutting in the middle of June and leave the foliage to grow to fern to enrich the roots for next year's crop.

BEANS

BROAD BEAN

A treble-purpose plant. Break off 8 cm or so (about 3 in) of the growing tips (**2**) when the bottom truss of flowers begins to turn into tiny pods. Use them as spinach. Baby pods can be cooked and eaten whole while the pods are still stringless. For shelling, pick them regularly to ensure a heavier crop, and on the young side, before they go starchy and the beans develop a black eye.

DWARF AND CLIMBING BEANS

Pick young and regularly to prevent the seeds from maturing and swelling in the pods. It also encourages more flowering shoots (**3** and **4**).

Don't feel guilty if your globe artichokes go to seed when your back is turned or you are on holiday. They become majestic purplish blue, thistle-like flowers which can be used fresh in flower arrangements, or dried and used in their natural state, or sprayed gold or silver for Christmas. Be sparing if you're tempted to snip pieces of asparagus fern to dress up sweet peas etc. for your vases; the fern is the lifeblood of next year's asparagus spears.

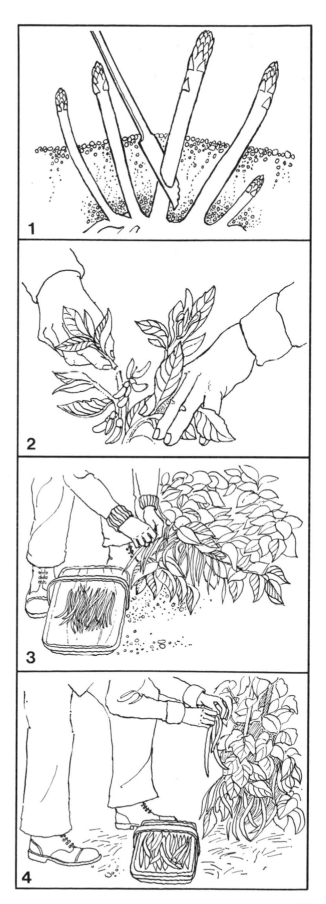

BEETROOT

A dual-purpose plant. Take a few leaves from each plant at a time to cook as spinach. The leaves of golden beet have the best flavour. Pull the early roots when they are the size of a golf ball (**1**). The white variety has the sweetest flavour and the red, the most earthy. Later roots may be stored in November, or covered with straw, bracken or cloches till needed during winter.

BROCCOLI

HEADING

Cut the white curds as soon as they are ready and before they start to open up (**2**). If a number of heads are ready together, delay cutting some of them by breaking two or three of the larger leaves over the curds for protection. Alternatively, pull up some that are ready for use and hang them upside down in a frostproof shed. The length of time they will keep depends on conditions; usually about 3 weeks. Keep an eye on them so they do not spoil.

SPROUTING

The flowering shoots grow out from in between the axils of the leaves. When these are about 22 cm (9in) long, snap or cut them off to within around 10–12 cm (a few inches) of their base (**3**). More shoots are then produced on the remaining stem. Do not remove the main leaves until they turn yellow, for they protect the delicate shoots. It is possible to have eaten almost the entire plant by the end of its season.

BRUSSELS SPROUTS

Yellowing of the lower leaves is a sign that the first sprouts are ready. Pick from the bottom of the stem, taking a few from each plant (**4**). Snap them off by pressing down sharply with the thumb. Any lower leaves in the way can be removed at the same time to help the remaining sprouts to develop. The leafy tops can be cut off and used as cabbage when the best of the button sprouts have been taken, and any loose 'blown' sprouts allowed to shoot. These stems, broken off where still tender, must be picked while the buds are still tight, and make a delicious novelty as 'sprout tops'. Left-overs are excellent served cold with a French dressing. All that should be left of a sprout plant is a naked stem . . . which, chopped up . . . feeds the compost heap.

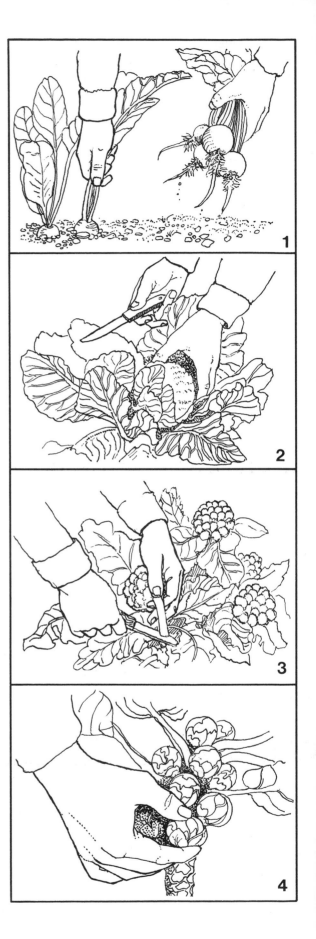

CABBAGE

Cut when they have a firm heart – according to type (**1**). Always pull up the stalks as soon as possible after cutting so that the ground is not robbed.

CHINESE CABBAGE

When it has 'hearted-up', cut whole and use as lettuce or cabbage. The outside leaves are best used boiled or steamed; they have the advantage that they never have that 'cabbage' smell when cooking.

CARROT

Pull the early varieties when young and tender (**2**) but large enough to have flavour. Lift the main crop before autumn and winter frosts (**3**), cut off the leaves and store in a box, as described in storing and preserving (**4**).

CAULIFLOWER

As for heading broccoli (see previous page), but cut the curds as early in the morning as possible, while they are moist with dew.

When freezing cauliflower (use only heads that are firm, compact and white), break into small sprigs and add the juice of a lemon to the blanching water, to prevent them discolouring. For freezing purposes, celeriac needs to be cooked until almost tender, peeled and sliced.

CELERY

SELF-BLANCHING

The sticks are usually ready for use at the end of August. As each is removed fill in the space with straw or other material, to keep light from the remaining plants (**1**). Use immediately as it does not keep well. Self-blanching celery is not hardy and all the crop must be cleared before the first serious frosts.

NON-SELF-BLANCHING

The first sticks should be sufficiently blanched and ready for use about two months after the first earthing up. As each celery plant is dug up for use, The soil must be replaced (**2**) so that the neighbouring plant will not be exposed to light and turn green.

CELERIAC

The roots will be small until they start to swell in late September or October; you can start to harvest them as soon as this occurs (**3**). In warmer parts of the country they can be left in the ground, covered with bracken or straw and dug up during winter as needed. Elsewhere, lift all roots before the frost arrives and store in sand in an airy shed.

CUCUMBER, ridge

Cut them regularly, as soon as they reach usable size, so that the plants will keep cropping (**4**). Never let them get too old or they will be fit only for the compost heap. If you leave them to grow, the plant will devote its energies to ripening the seed rather than producing more new growth and flowers. Ridge cucumbers store well, provided they are kept in a cool place. Stack them on racks or on a brick or stone floor.

Should your ridge cucumbers produce such a heavy crop that you cannot use them all, peel them, and liquidise in a blender, then freeze to use in iced soups or sauces.

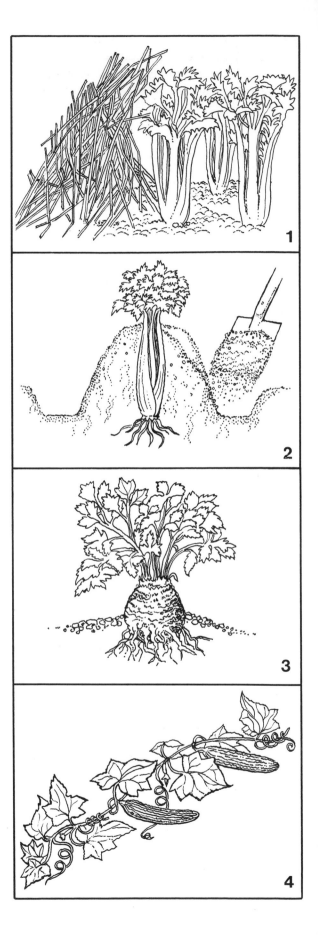

KOHLRABI

This vegetable must be used when young for perfection – about 5 cm (2 in) in diameter (**1**). The stems will swell to a much larger size but become coarse and inedible. The young ones can be scrubbed and cooked whole, the middle-aged are best peeled thickly, and the ancient are fit only for compost. Plants may be left in the ground until needed and can withstand quite hard frost; they will keep for only a short time if stored. Usually ready to harvest between July and November.

LEEK

Begin using as soon as they are large enough to suit your purpose. Dig as required, the soil being put back in position to keep the other stems white. They are hardy and can be left in the ground over winter. But if you need the ground to prepare for other crops, they can be lifted and heeled into a trench in a cool, sheltered place (**2, 3**).

MARROW

Cut as a rule when young and tender, or they will be thick-skinned. Regular cutting can treble the crop of a plant. If you want some large marrows to store for the winter, leave these to ripen from early September and cut them late in October.

ONION

The first sign of maturity is the foliage toppling over; this will vary with variety and weather conditions. Help them to ripen by bending the collapsing greenery neatly between the bulbs, so that the leaves will dry off. About 10 to 14 days later the onions may be lifted from the soil and left where they are on the surface to dry off (**4**). Turn them over 14 days later so they will ripen evenly, and two weeks later they should be ready to store.

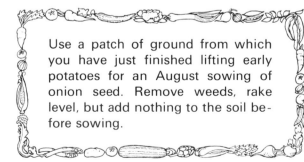

Use a patch of ground from which you have just finished lifting early potatoes for an August sowing of onion seed. Remove weeds, rake level, but add nothing to the soil before sowing.

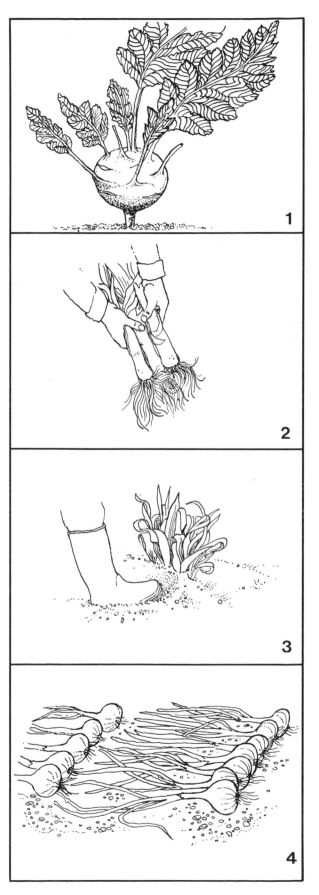

PARSNIP

They taste better when they have been touched by frost and can be dug up as they are needed (**1**). If there is any danger of the ground being frozen so hard that the roots cannot be lifted just when you want, an 'iron ration' quantity can be dug up and stored for a frosty day.

PEAS

Pick while there is some 'give' when you press the pod (**2**), and the peas have not become so large that they have taken up all the inner space. Pick regularly and be careful to remove all the pods that are ready. If only one or two are accidentally left to ripen their seeds, the quantity of the crop will be sadly reduced.

POTATO

The earliest can be lifted in June or July as soon as they are large enough; this is usually when they are beginning to flower. Don't be tempted to dig up the whole crop while they are small – it can double its weight in two weeks. Never plunge the fork straight into the ground and risk impaling some of the precious crop, but fork on the side to throw the plants forward (**3**). Special flat-tined forks can be bought if you grow enough to justify the expense.

Lift the main crop when the haulm (the strawy stem) has died down in October. Cut off the tops and put on the compost heap before digging up the main crop. There is then no fear that spores of any disease on the leaves will drop down on to the potatoes themselves and cause trouble when they are stored. Choose a fine day and leave the tubers on the ground for a few hours to dry (**4**). Then put all the sound, undamaged ones in paper or hessian bags and store in a dark, frostproof place.

Don't worry if the seed potato bought in a pack seems disappointing, with the tubers large, small and indifferent. It's worth taking a chance and going ahead and planting them; results from scruffy-looking tubers are often superior to those of regular shape and features.

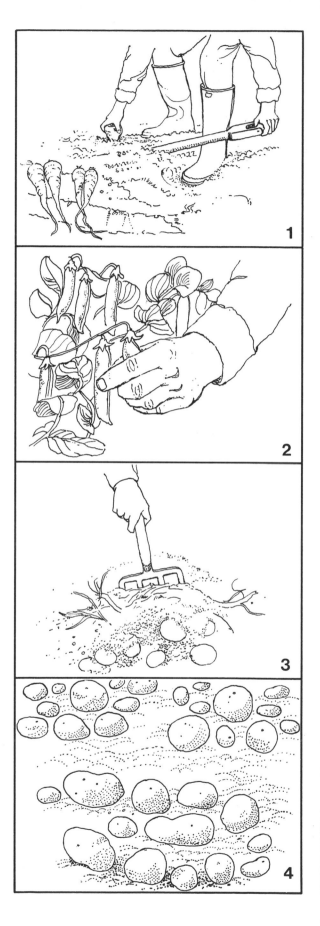

SALSIFY

The roots will be ready for use in the autumn, towards the end of October. They can be left in the ground all winter and dug when needed, or stored. Take great care not to damage the roots in lifting or they will 'bleed'. If some roots are still left in the ground in spring, tender shoots can be taken in March or April and used green, or blanched, in salads (**1**).

SEAKALE BEET

A dual-purpose vegetable. Pull off the stem and leaf in one piece (**2**) regularly as they become ready in summer and autumn; take a few outside leaves from each plant. Some plants live through the winter and will send up more leaves again in spring. Never strip off the green leaves leaving the white stems on the plant or they will rot back and cause trouble. These are the seakale part of the plant, and are cooked separately from the green leaves which are used as spinach (see page 84).

SHALLOTS

In June, scrape some soil away from the bulb clusters to expose them to the light and help them to ripen (**3**); they should be ready to harvest sometime in July. Wait for a sunny day about two weeks after the leaves start to turn yellow. Lift the clusters carefully with a fork and leave them on the surface to dry. A week later put the clusters on a path (not grass) or any hard surface to continue ripening, turning them a few times.

After about a week of this treatment they can be divided into separate bulbs (**4**) and hung up in a dry, cool shed. They should not be left on the ground as they store better with a good air circulation.

> Don't keep your shallots just for pickling; used fresh in cooking they have a more delicate flavour than the onion and are much used in French cooking. Reserve some of the most healthy, medium-sized bulbs for re-planting for the next season's crop.

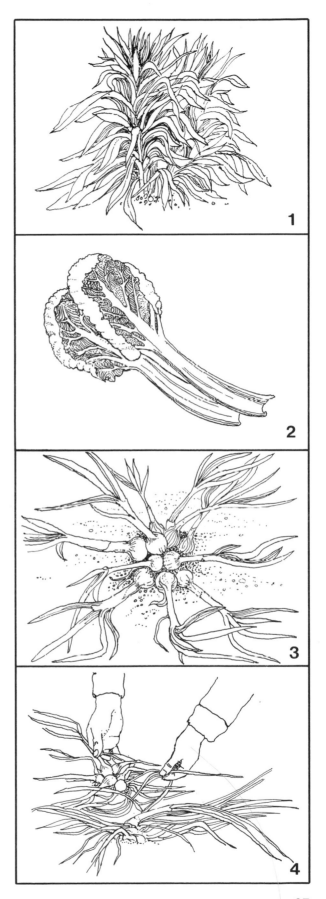

SPINACH

SUMMER

Always pull the leaves when young and tender and not too large. Pick regularly and fairly hard. You can pick most of the leaves from the plants leaving only a few in position to continue the growth (**1**).

WINTER

This should not be picked hard or the plants will spoil. Take only the largest leaves and only a few from each plant. They die at the end of winter.

SPINACH BEET

Pick the leaves when they are ready (**2**) and don't leave them to grow large and old. Pick regularly, even when not wanted for the table (failing a neighbour who would be glad of them, they can be fed to the compost heap) to ensure that new leaves will grow in place of the old ones. Plants from an autumn sowing should be allowed to build themselves up well before winter really sets in; pick fewer leaves from them.

SWEET CORN

When the silks at the top of the cobs start to dry and turn brown, ripening has started. To test when ready, part the outer sheath with thumbnails at the fattest part. The grains should look pale yellow but fully developed. Expert advice varies here. Most say 'pop' the grain with thumb or knife and the liquid should be like clotted cream, neither runny nor cheesy. As this operation spoils the appearance of the cooked cob, it is better done at the top rather than the fat middle, but remember that the grains at the base will be more mature. Cobs taken too early will be watery; those too late, hard, starchy and unpalatable. Break or twist them off with a downward pull (**3**) and cook within an hour at most.

When more cobs of corn ripen to perfection-point than the family can possibly digest, pick and cook them at once. Drain immediately under cold running water. Then dry and keep in Polythene bags in the refrigerator, or remove grains with a sharp knife first. This saves space and makes the corn more adaptable for a variety of dishes than if left on the cob. If not to be eaten within a few days they must be frozen.

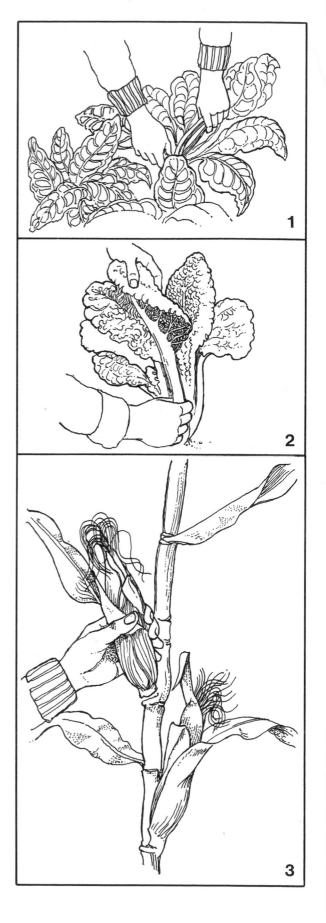

TOMATO (OUTDOORS)

Use the fruit as it ripens (**1**). If it has to be picked before it is fully ripe owing to attacks from blackbirds and thrushes, the ripening can be continued indoors.

If there are still trusses of green tomatoes at the end of the season, cut them off to ripen the fruit on a sunny windowsill (**2**). If you prefer you can hang the trusses in a frost-free shed. See also page 73 for other methods; whichever you choose, remember to take a look at them frequently.

TURNIP

The early varieties must be pulled when the roots are young and fresh (**3**); never let them get coarse or go to seed.

The winter varieties can stay in the ground and be used as they are needed (**4**). Or they can be lifted in November and, when the tops have been cut off, stored in the same way as potatoes

Gardeners without cloches can still get a good start by sowing seed under glass jars. Sow three seeds at intervals of 38 cm (15 in) at a depth of from 1–3 cm ($\frac{1}{2}$–1 in or so). The lighter and sandier the soil, the deeper you may sow. Cover with fine soil, then invert the glass jar on top. When they germinate, choose the strongest seedling to grow on, and pinch out the others. Take off the jars before the seedlings outgrow them. Put the jars back at night if there is any threat of frost.

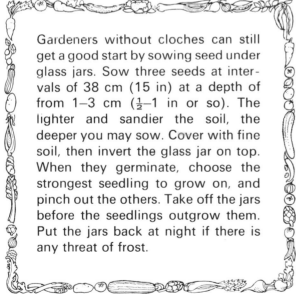

Storing and Preserving

There is little point in growing vegetables for winter which are ruined by careless storing. It is just a *double* waste of time and effort.

There are various different methods and techniques of storing, ranging from racks and shelves, boxes, wire trays, sacks, sand, peat and nets to old-fashioned clamps and 'pies' (see below and opposite). Even old nylon tights or stockings can be put to good use at harvest time.

Golden rule Never store anything which is not in perfect health, as rot or disease will spread quickly.

Danger signs Onions: softness, specially round the neck, or black areas on the bulbs.
Carrots: scored by fly maggots.
Parsnips: soft dark areas of canker.
Any root vegetable with skin damaged in lifting: the skin is the insulation. This also applies to marrows and tomatoes.

MAKING A CLAMP OR 'PIE'
This cheap and simple method gives complete protection, however severe the winter. Use a well-protected, well-drained part of the garden. Put down a layer of dry straw or clinker about 1.50 m (5 ft) wide. Build the roots into a broad-based, tapering heap (**1**). Cover the heap with a 15 cm (6 in) thickness of straw and leave the roots to sweat for a few days (**2**). Then cover the straw and the whole heap with a layer of packed soils of the same depth, made smooth and firm by patting with the back of a spade. The heap must be entirely soil-crusted apart from a tuft of straw at the peak to act as a chimney and ventilator (**3**). To cover the clamp use soil from around it, to make a drainage trench around the base (**4**). This will prevent the bottom of the clamp becoming waterlogged in wet weather.

Caution This system is best where a large quantity of roots have to be stored, and when a good number can be taken out at a time. A clamp is not something you want to open every day, like the refrigerator. To remove moderate quantities you plunge a hand down the 'chimney'. For large sorties, the 'pie crust' is broken into and replaced.

Disadvantages The clamp cannot be opened during a frost, without risk to the stored roots.

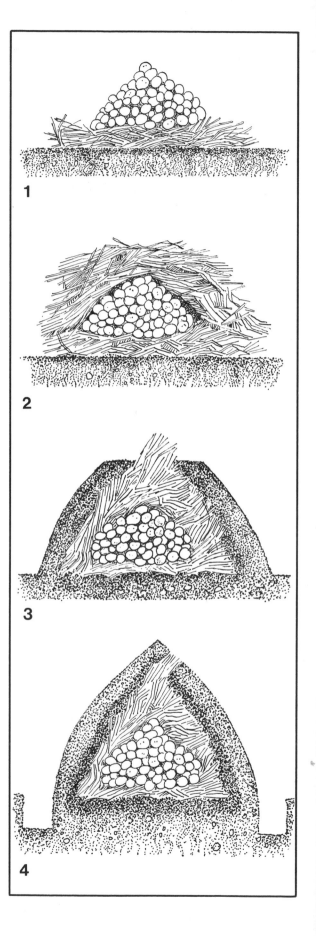

Here are some tips on storing certain individual vegetables. (Storing methods are also referred to briefly in the Harvesting section.)

BEETROOT

Twist off the tops leaving about 5 cm (2 in) of leaf stalk. This reduces 'bleeding' which occurs if the leaves are cut off. Line a deep box with 2–3 cm (1 in) slightly damp sand or peat, put in a layer of roots (**1**), followed by a layer of sand and so on. Keep the boxes in a dry, cool, frostproof place, and watch out for mice. The sand, peat or other storing material should not be overwet; just suffcient to stop shrivelling but not enough to cause rotting or encourage fresh growth. Beet can also be 'pied' (see previous page).

CARROT

As for beetroot, except tops are cut off close to the head and the roots laid head to tail (**2**).

CELERIAC, CUCUMBER

See page 64.

KOHLRABI

Late-sown ones can be left in the ground and used as wanted, or lifted and stored in the same way as beetroot and carrots.

MARROW

The skins must be hard for storing purposes. Marrows can be stored on a shelf in a well-ventilated, frostproof place, or hung up in netting (**3**), string bags or anything which will let the air circulate around them.

ONION

These must be stored so the air can move freely between them. They can be placed on slatted, wooden trays, wire-based boxes (**4**), or strung up in ropes. Hang up a stout length of thin rope or strong twine to a pole or beam in a shed or garage. Pull off the roots and tie the necks round the cord. If the neck is too short, use string or raffia. Stop before the 'rope' of roots is too heavy to carry about. Keep one rope handy, in or near the kitchen, and the rest in a dry, ventilated, frostproof place.

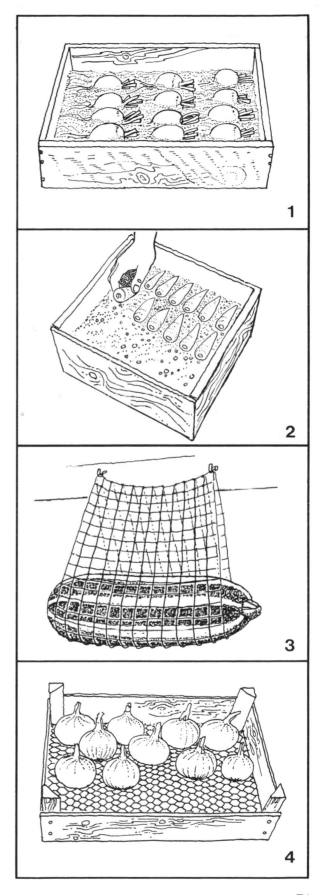

Alternatively, use old nylon stockings or tights (the ladders or holes will ensure ventilation). Put the onions down the legs, tying a knot between each one (**1**). Cut them off as you want them, below a knot.

PARSNIP

If they cannot be left in the ground, dig them up and leave in a heap where the frost can touch and sweeten them and the rain can wash them clean (**2**). In the north, where frosts are longer and harder, it is advisable to put them under cover with a sack over them.

POTATO

Large quantities can be stored in 'pies' (see page 70). Put small quantities in orange boxes lined with straw and topped with more straw or newspapers, to stop the tubers from going green. Or they can be kept in slatted trays (**3**); top with material to keep out the light. Sacks of hessian, paper, or plastic are other alternatives.

Caution: The roots must be allowed to 'sweat' for a few days before being bagged, and must be inspected regularly for mice and rotting. Make small holes in plastic and paper sacks so the potatoes can breathe.

LATE 'NEW' POTATO

A worthwhile method to ensure a New Year feast. In September keep aside any small paper-thin-skinned tubers when digging up roots for daily use. Put them, clean and dry, into a biscuit tin lined with sawdust or peat. Don't let the roots touch, and cover each layer. Seal the lid with adhesive tape and bury the tin with a few inches of soil on top (**4**). Remember to mark the spot!

Sprout seed potatoes, where space is short, by threading them on strong twine or string with a coarse darning needle. Hang them in the kitchen, bathroom or any convenient place where there is a reasonable amount of light and a temperature of about 10°C (50°F).

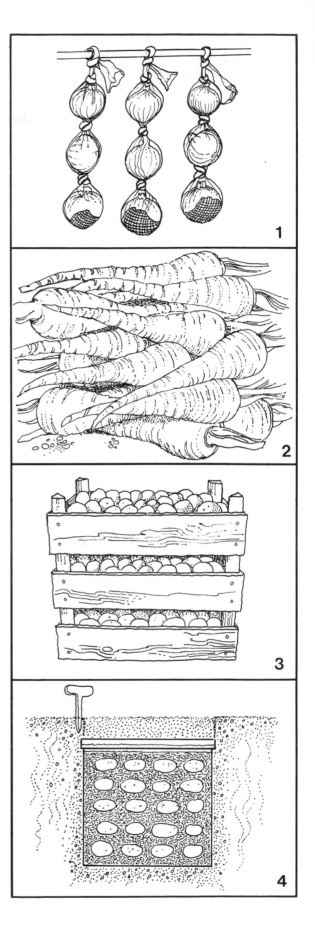

SALSIFY

If they cannot be left in the ground until needed, store in layers of sand or peat (**1**).

SHALLOTS

Separate bulbs, take off the dried outer skin, leaves etc. (**2**) and store as for onions on wire or wooden trays and racks. They are rather fiddley to 'rope'.

TOMATO

Whole green trusses can be hung in a frost-free place which need not be dark (**3**). Alternatively, the fruit can be kept on trays under a bed or in a cupboard, or in drawers lined with newspapers. Much depends on their condition when harvested. If you want them quickly, keep them in slight warmth. If you want them for Christmas, keep them cool but frost-free and bring a few at a time into the warmth. Place them in a wide fruit bowl in the living room; the ripe tomatoes will help to ripen the green ones among them.

TURNIP

As for beetroot, carrots and potatoes (**4**).

Turnip tops are a useful form of green vegetable in spring. Sow the seed fairly thickly in August in shallow drills about 0.50 m (1 ft 6 in) apart for a supply the following spring. Take only a few leaves from each plant when picking for the table.

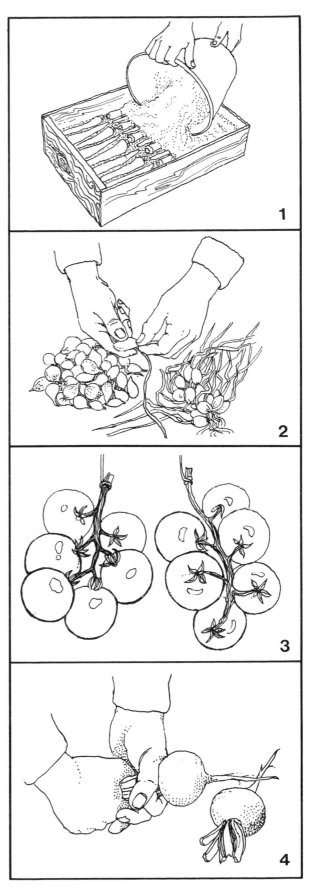

MOST VALUABLE CROPS FOR FREEZING

(Short season or glut vegetables)

BEANS, BROAD
All varieties; exceptionally good are:
Masterpiece
Dreadnought
Red Epicure

BEANS, DWARF, BUSH AND CLIMBING
Remus
Royalty
Fry
Romano

BROCCOLI
Purple and white sprouting
Calabrese

BRUSSELS SPROUTS
Focus 1
British All-rounder
Prince Astrol
Peer Gynt

Cauliflower
Chinese Cabbage
Early Carrots
Globe Artichoke   *All varieties are*
Kale   *equally suitable*
Summer Spinach

MARROWS
Courgette
Zucchini
Cocozelle
Gold Nugget

PEAS
Hurst's Green Shaft
Victory Freezer
Recette
Gloriosa

SWEET CORN
Kelvedon Glory
North Star Hybrid

Note: The catalogues of leading seedsmen mark·
varieties which are specially good for freezing.

Monthly Reminders

JANUARY

Burn up everything which cannot be composted. Store the cold ashes in sacks to use later in the year; spread them on the compost heap, or on ground where you intend to grow broad beans.

Make a plan of the garden, referring to last year's plan so that crops will be rotated (see page 11). Remember that two years at least should elapse before the same family occupies the same site.

Complete digging and leave the ground rough so that frost, wind and rain can break it into crumbs – a process known as 'weathering' (see page 10).

Study catalogues and make seed lists, to order.

Check your supplies of seed boxes, labels, seed compost etc. and order more when necessary, so that you do not run out of them during a busy time.

FEBRUARY

Put seed potatoes to sprout in a light, airy, frost-proof place (see page 27). Stand them on end in shallow boxes or trays (egg cartons are ideal). Turn them around if shoots grow underneath. If you have cloches plant some of the sprouted ones 10 cm (4 in) deep, 30 cm (1 ft) apart, having removed all but say three of the stronger sprouts. A few early ones will be more appreciated than a lot of later ones. Lift a root of mint and plant it inside one end of the row to be ready at the same time as the tubers.

Rub off any sprouts which develop on stored potatoes or any other stored vegetables (**right**).

Plant Jerusalem artichoke and shallots.

Sow in the open towards the end of the month: parsnip, broad bean, early peas and round-seeded (summer) spinach and a little cabbage.

Have a relentless spring clean among the brassicas. If the weather is mild they will start to flower. Rescue what you can for the deep freeze. Pull up all stumps that are finished. Put soft parts on the compost heap; cut up and compost the stems or burn them. Rake out dead leaves and debris and fork over the ground.

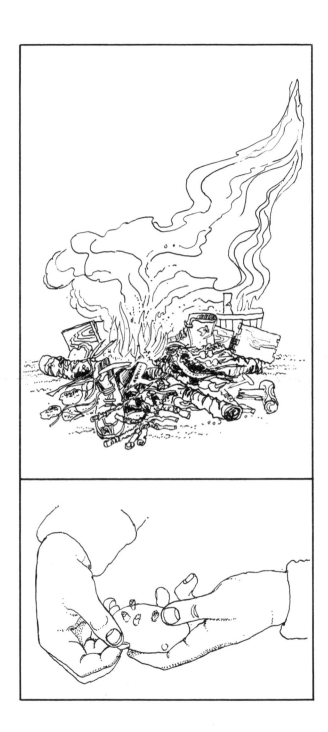

MARCH

It is not practicable to give any hard and fast advice as to when to sow in the open during this month. It depends entirely on locality and individual soil conditions. If it is still wet and cold, you are wasting time and money in trying to sow, unless cloches have been used.

Prepare soil for seed sowing (see page 13), making it firm, level and fine; neither too wet nor too dry.

Sow in nursery beds: cabbage, Savoy, Brussels sprouts, heading broccoli, cauliflower for transplanting later.

Sow in the open garden where they are to crop: early peas, carrot, radish, turnip, parsley, spinach, onion, lettuce, parsnip.

Sow in slight heat or under cloches: celery, celeriac, tomato, leek, lettuce, and anything you appreciate particularly early.

Plant Jerusalem artichoke, asparagus, early potato, shallot.

Dig up mint and replant in a new bed. This keeps it under control and prevents rust. If only a small quantity is needed plant it in an old bottomless bucket so the roots cannot wander (**below**).

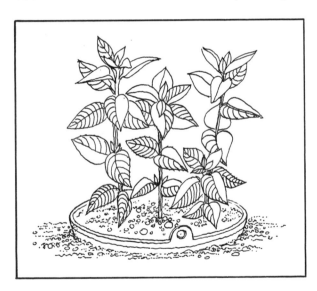

If winter greens and leek are taking up room wanted for sowing or planting, dig them up and heel them in (see page 24) where you can get at them easily. This saves space, stops them from bolting, and will keep you supplied for several more weeks.

APRIL

Sow in the open: beetroot, brassicas (see page 12), carrot, kohlrabi, leek, lettuce, onion, parsley, parsnip, mid-season peas, salsify, seakale beet, spinach, spinach beet, turnip, all main crops leaving runner and French beans till the following month.

Sow in the slight heat or under cloches: runner bean, celery, ridge cucumber, sweetcorn, tomato, marrow.

Plant artichokes (globe and Jerusalem), asparagus, mint, onion sets, potato.

Harden off seedlings under glass before planting out.

Prepare celery trenches.

Treat onion seedlings with Calomel dust.

Pull up any remaining winter greenstuff before it flowers.

Burn any roots which are swollen or unhealthy.

Earth up early potato.

MAY

Complete planting of early potato.

Plant out sprouts and cauliflower, also leek and celery.

Sow French and runner beans, late peas, turnip, kale, beetroot, salads, sweetcorn, parsley, summer spinach, spinach beet, marrow.

Sow in a seedbed for winter use: broccoli, winter cabbage, kale, Savoy.

Prepare the ground for the main planting out of tomatoes and marrow.

Protect all young crops from slugs, particularly those newly planted out.

Spray potatoes with Bordeaux mixture or Zineb (see pages 58–59) as a guard against blight.

Prepare for planting out brassicas (see page 12) next month by treading or rolling the bed to make it firm, but not airless; do it only when the ground is dry.

Prepare celery bed ready by working in manure or compost.

Dig ground recently cleared of a late green crop and prepare for leek.

JUNE

Finish planting out all seedlings raised under glass.

Stop cutting asparagus in the middle of the month.

Sow beans, beetroot, carrot, kale, lettuce, marrow, peas.

Plant beans, celery, leek, marrow, tomato, brassicas. Remember that sprouts need particularly well-firmed ground.

Thin beetroot, carrot, lettuce, turnip.

Stake or support runner bean.

Pinch out tops of broad bean when in full flower.

Hoe, thin and water all young growing crops.

Watch out for pests and diseases and catch them at an early stage (see pages 51–58).

JULY

Lift early potato and plant out more winter greens in the vacant ground.

Plant celery in trenches, celeriac, broccoli, kales, winter cabbage, leek.

Sow spring cabbage, winter lettuce, turnip, carrot, salads, and in some regions a last sowing of peas and French bean.

Water celery (**below**), globe artichoke, marrow and runner bean when necessary.

Remove side growths from single-stemmed tomato and keep them well supported.

Protect cauliflower curds from the sun by breaking off or bending over leaves from the plant (see page 22).

Pinch out the growing points of climbing beans when they have reached the tops of their poles or supports (see page 20).

Hoe to keep down weeds and aerate the soil.

Feed crops with liquid fertiliser (see page 48).

Earth up the shallow roots of sweetcorn and also stake them if your garden is exposed, to stop the roots from being shaken and so upsetting the growing and ripening process (**right**).

Watch tomato for blight.

Examine the hearts of young brassica (see page 12) for the grey mealy aphis and spray with Derris. Dust young turnip with Derris powder to deter flea beetle (see page 54).

AUGUST

Plant out kale and Savoys.

Remove suckers from base of celery plants, tie the plants and soak the trench thoroughly before earthing up for the first time, drawing the soil up only a few inches.

Bend over onion tops to encourage ripening.

Sow cauliflower, spring cabbage, radish, parsley, spinach beet and winter spinach.

Stop tomato plants when four trusses of fruit have set (see page 33).

Support French bean and keep ridge cucumber and all the marrow family from direct contact with the ground, to prevent damage by insects and to keep them from rotting.

Harvest runner bean and sweetcorn before they get coarse or tough; shallot when they become golden brown.

Plant the latest green crops as early as possible in the month, to make use of all the ground available.

SEPTEMBER

Sow winter lettuce, winter spinach and turnip – for use as turnip tops as well as roots.

Plant spring cabbage at the end of the month.

Earth up celery and leek.

Lift and store onion.

Cut down asparagus foliage and give the bed a good mulch of compost or well-rotted manure.

Pull up tomato plants at the end of the month and store (see page 73).

Watch out for cabbage caterpillars and celery leaf maggot (see pages 52–53).

OCTOBER

Lift and store root crops.

Earth up celery for the last time (see pages 23, 64) and continue earthing up leek.

Thin winter spinach to 15 cm (6 in) apart.

Put cloches over autumn-sown lettuce (**right**).

Hoe, if possible between all crops, especially spring cabbage, winter onion, lettuce and spinach, to stand the winter (**centre, right**).

Start using self-blanching celery.

Remove all spent crops at once, especially the stumps of cabbages and cauliflowers which could harbour pests and disease.

Burn diseases or hard materials which will not rot down in the compost heap; add the ashes to the compost before rain washes it into the soil on which it is built.

Start a separate heap of leaves for leafmould.

NOVEMBER

Sow broad bean if your ground is not too heavy or exposed. It's a gamble, but if they survive the winter they will be more forward than even cloche-raised ones, in the spring, and will have finished cropping before they are attacked by blackfly. Sow a long-pod variety such as *Dreadnought* as these are hardier than *Windsor*. Space the seed 7–10 cm (3–4 in) apart in flat-bottomed drills. Alternatively, sow directly onto a firm, well-prepared surface, with a 5 cm (2 in) thick layer of compost, earth, or wood ash on top (wood ash helps to keep mice away). Protect the stems during winter by drawing earth or leaves up to the growing tips.

Pull off yellowing leaves of brassica plants.

Lift Jerusalem artichoke as wanted.

DECEMBER

Dig and manure all ground which is cleared, and lime where necessary.

Examine root crops in store.

Order seed potato and Jerusalem artichoke.

Send for seed catalogues.

Protect celery and globe artichoke with straw or bracken and increase the protective material of outdoor clamps if severe frost is threatened (**right**).

Tips on Preparation and Cooking

GOLDEN RULES

1 Gather vegetables from the garden as close as possible to the moment you are going to use them.
2 Leave on outer leaves, roots and tops till you are ready to prepare or cook, to preserve vitamins.
3 Wash or scrub them rapidly under a cold tap. Leaving vegetables to soak or the use of warm water destroys vitamins A, c and e.
4 Avoid peeling if possible. Many valuable nutrients lie directly under the skin.

ARTICHOKE

GLOBE

Cut off the stem close to the base and remove outer layer of leaves. Wash thoroughly under a strong jet of water to flush out any earwigs or other insects. Boil in salted water 20–40 minutes according to size; leaves pull off easily when cooked. Drain upside down (**above, right**) and serve hot with melted butter or cold with vinaigrette dressing.

JERUSALEM

Scrub rapidly, and keep covered in the refrigerator if not to be cooked at once. This helps to keep their sugar content. Always steam or boil gently in salted water in their skins, which should be pulled off just before serving; otherwise they will lose much of their goodness. Be careful not to over-cook – they should be just soft, not mushy. Very good parboiled in their skins then peeled, tossed in seasoned flour, coated with batter, deep-foiled and served very hot with melted butter.

ASPARAGUS

Try to use not more than half an hour after cutting. If this is impossible stand the stems upright in about 5 cm (2 in) depth of water. Break off the ends where they snap easily and use these for soup or stock. Cook gently so that the tips receive less heat than the thick ends. This can be done by tying them in bundles and standing them in water up to their necks, so that the bottoms boil and the tips steam (about 20 minutes). Or you can use a long shallow pan of water, laying the stems lengthways with the

thick ends simmering and the tips off the heat. This can be achieved by laying a wooden spoon or some kind of wedge under the tips so they are raised above the water and are steamed (**below**, page 79).

BEANS

BROAD

Use tips as spinach, see page 61 (**right**). Cook pods whole when they are about 5 cm (2 in) long and the beans the size of peas. If any pods become over-mature so that the beans have developed black eyes, boil them until you can slip off the outer skins and discard them. A little fiddley as it must be done while they are hot, but they are delicious served warm, on the spot, or heated up later in melted butter or parsley sauce.

FRENCH AND RUNNER

Best used when young and stringless. If you are unable to harvest all of them at the perfect moment and the beans begin to swell, they can be shelled and used in the same way as shelled peas. In late summer, when pulling the spent plants for the compost heap, pull off any pods which have escaped your eye and started to dry. They can be shelled and used as haricot beans, or left to dry further under cover and used as seed the following year.

BEETROOT

Do not peel or scrape or they will 'bleed'. Boil in salted water until soft (about 2 hours) or bake whole, sprinkled with salt, in a cool oven until cooked. Leave to go cold then rub off the skin. Beet tops can be used as spinach (see page 62.) Freshly pulled young globe beetroot have more flavour and take less time to cook than stored beetroot. Make use of them during summer when they are fresh and sweet. Very young thinnings – no thicker than your thumb – can be washed and cooked whole with their tops on.

BROCCOLI

HEADING

Best steamed as boiling damages much of their flavour. This is mostly contained in the white stems, which may need peeling. If the head is to be used whole, split the stem several times so it will cook faster (**right**). As the 'flower' needs less cooking, put the vegetable, stem down, in a saucepan containing boiling water to the depth of about 5 cm (2 in) and tilt the lid, so that the stem boils and the head steams.

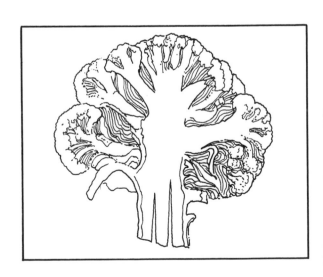

80

SPROUTING
The first thick shoots can be cooked like asparagus. As more thinner side shoots appear they can be steamed or boiled.

BROCCOLI LEAVES
The young, smaller ones can be washed and simmered in a little oil in a lidded saucepan until tender. Keep the heat very low. Turn occasionally with a slice and add salt only at the end (**right**). The same treatment can be given to any young leaves – cauliflower, sprout tops, radish, beet, turnip tops.

BRUSSELS SPROUTS
Try cooking the tight, baby ones in very little boiling water, with a large lump of butter or bacon fat; cover and boil fast till all liquid has evaporated and they still have a slight crunch to them. Don't leave the kitchen in case the butter starts to burn. Brussels sprout tops are a special delicacy (see page 62).

CARROT
Brush well but avoid scraping or peeling, unless there are diseased or damaged parts to cut out, as the outer part is the most valuable. Cook the baby ones whole. When slicing carrots, cut them on a bias (**right**), not straight – they cook better. Best flavour is achieved by steaming, or by using just enough water to cover the bottom of the pan, a pinch of salt and sugar, and large lump of butter; cover the pan and cook over a gentle heat, shaking occasionally until tender, but not too soft. To be used raw they should be grated only just before serving or much of their goodness will be wasted.

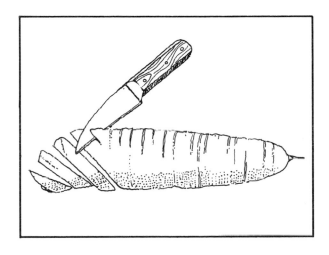

CHINESE CABBAGE
Slice them diagonally and use as you would lettuce or cabbage. These can grow rather large and if there is too much to use at once, cut off what you need and leave the rest in a dry polythene bag in the salad drawer of the refrigerator.

CAULIFLOWER
As for heading broccoli, but cut the curds as early as possible in the morning when they are still damp with dew. Put them in a dark, cold place till you use them – preferably the same day.

CELERY
Keep the outer stalks to flavour soup and stock. Don't cut off all the root – it's delicious grated or chopped raw in salad.

CELERIAC

Not the easiest of vegetables to prepare because of its uneven shape. After washing it well, cut it into thick slices and *then* peel it (**right**). Good used raw as an hors d'oeuvre or in salads. Also good as a hot vegetable, fritters or as soup.

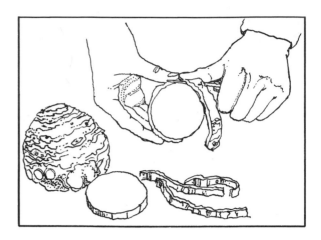

CUCUMBER, ridge

Apart from their use in salads, they can be cooked as a delicate hot vegetable, stuffed with meat and braised, or used to make a refreshing cold soup.

KOHLRABI

Must be quickly grown and used when small. Boil for about half an hour or steam, preferably with the skin on; remove the skin before serving. They can be steamed, then sliced, dipped in butter and fried; or grated raw into salads. A good tip for a party is to peel them, cut them into rings and use them raw as bases on which to spread cocktail savouries (**right**).

LEEK

The best way to get them clean when they are to be used whole is to cut off roots and most of green part (the tenderest part of the green can be used for soup); then make a nick down either side of the tops for about 5 cm (2 in) and stand them upside down in water for at least half an hour. You will be surprised at the dirt which sinks to the bottom (**below, right**).

Any seedlings which were not seeded for planting out make a delightful hors d'oeuvre or salad. Boil them in very little water and let them cool in it. Drain off and blend the liquor with a little cornflour. Stir over gentle heat until the sauce thickens. Squeeze in the juice of a lemon, add a tablespoon of olive oil and let the leeks cool in the sauce.

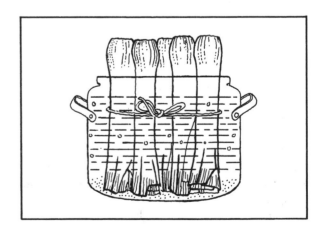

MARROW

Since they consist largely of water, boiling is the least satisfactory method of cooking marrow; frying in a little butter or baking is preferable. Pick them very young and cook them in their skins, where most of the flavour lies. When using them halved or sliced, sprinkle the cut sides with salt, and leave weighted down in a colander or towel, for at least an hour to extract some of the liquid. Pat dry before cooking.

ONION

Some stored onions inevitably start to sprout towards the end of the winter (**right**), particularly after a mild one. There is no need to banish them to the compost heap. Peel off the outer layers of the bulb which have gone soft, and use the tender white inside and green tops as you would spring onions.

PARSNIP

Not worth eating until they have been sweetened by frost. Give them a good scrub, leave on the skin, then dry. They are at their best roast after parboiling for a few minutes in salted water, or 'chipped' like potatoes. This treatment is not suitable once they are no longer young, when they need to be peeled, sliced and boiled for about half an hour and then tossed in butter.

PEAS

Must be used within a few hours of picking, and cooked immediately after shelling; they start to lose their sweetness the moment they leave the plant so speed from plant to cooking pan is essential. If you cannot use them at once, pick them at a time you can shell them immediately and cook them (never overcook). Run cold water over them until they are quite cold, drain, and keep covered in the refrigerator until you are ready to eat them. Re-heat them gently in melted butter and serve at once. This way of saving their lives retains all their original sweetness. Cooked peas can even be re-heated the following day.

SALSIFY

The roots are rather a trouble to clean. To keep them white they must be scraped quickly and put immediately into cold water with a good dash of lemon juice or vinegar. The roots can be washed and cooked whole, and the skins taken off while they are still hot. If fresh from the garden the skins will usually rub off with a cloth, though you may need a small knife for stored ones (**right**). Salsify is usually served with a white sauce, or parboiled, dipped in batter and fried in deep fat until crisp.

Any roots left in the ground over winter will produce green shoots in March. Cut these when about 15 cm (6 in) long and cook like spinach. The roots will go on producing these 'bonus' shoots till early June, so don't be in a hurry to dig them up unless the space is needed urgently. Their flavour has a hint of asparagus.

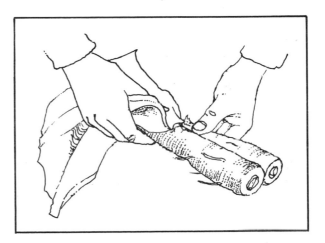

SEAKALE BEET

A two-in-one vegetable (see page 67) and particularly useful as it matures when other green vegetables are scarce. Cut out the white rib (**right**) to deal with separately (see below). Wash the green leaves under running water and cook in very little water like spinach, turning the leaves frequently.

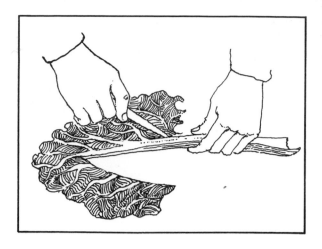

Mid-ribs: Cut into short even lengths and boil in water with a little lemon juice added to keep them white; serve with a white or cheese sauce. Or put them in a casserole with a very little water, a chopped onion and a knob of butter. Cover and cook slowly until tender – about 1 hour. Serve as it is or remove lid, sprinkle with grated cheese and breadcrumbs, dot with butter, and return to oven or put under grill to brown.

SWEET CORN

The golden rule is to have the water boiling in the pan before you break off the cobs. Remove silks, stem and sheaths (**right**). If as young and fresh as they should be (see page 68), they will need only 5–8 minutes cooking.

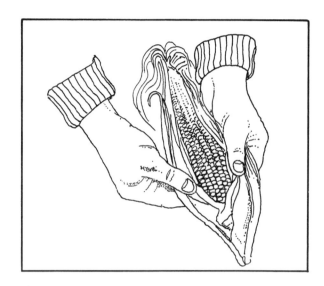

If they need picking urgently to save them from spoiling, cook as above. Cool them at once, and keep in the refrigerator until needed. They can be left whole or the grains cut off with a sharp knife. Those left on the cob can be reheated in butter, or buttered and grilled. The loose ones can be tossed gently in butter or are most useful additions to composite dishes or salads. They are specially good stirred into scrambled eggs, or in stuffed tomatoes.

TOMATO

The great advantage of growing your own is that you can pick them in exactly the condition you like them best – ripe, under-ripe or over-ripe – the last have the best flavour for soup and cooked dishes. Scald off the skins if they are tough. Put in a bowl, pour boiling water over them (**right**) and

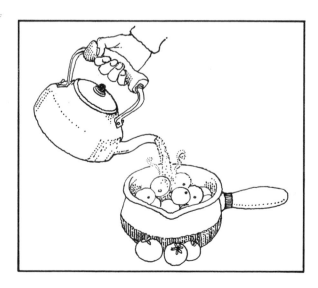

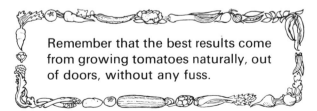

Remember that the best results come from growing tomatoes naturally, out of doors, without any fuss.

count up to 5 or 10, depending on the speed of your count and the ripeness of the tomatoes; the riper the tomato the shorter the time. Take one out and test quickly with the tip of a sharp knife where the fruit was attached to the stem. The skin should come off only one layer deep (**right**). If it rubs off with some of the fruit, you have scalded them for too long. Drain and plunge them straight into cold water so that they do not start to cook and ruin the flavour. It is a tricky but important operation and worth a little trial and error to master.

Small, whole tomatoes are a taste-bud experience if left to seep for half a day in a sprinkling of olive oil, sugar, salt, pepper and chopped sweet basil. Turn them over gently in their bowl with a spoon several times, and serve on their own with new bread.

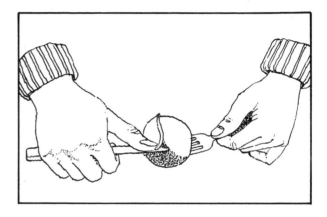

TURNIP

An absurdly abused vegetable, it is very often wrongly grown, wrongly harvested and horribly cooked. Turnips must grow quickly to be sweet (like radish), harvested small and eaten quickly. They can be quartered and eaten raw with salt. If you prefer them cooked, they can be grilled, baked or steamed in their skins. Wonderful partly steamed, then glazed in a pan of melted butter and soft brown sugar; shake them until they brown and serve with ham or duck (**right**). Larger turnips taken from the ground in winter, or from store, must be peeled and steamed or boiled. Good mashed with bacon fat.

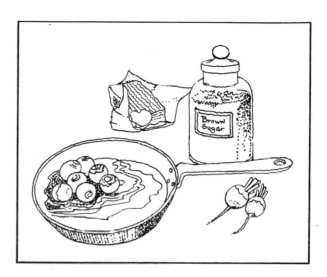

Index